PEACE IS ACTIVE

TOM McCANN

Little Creek Press
5341 Sunny Ridge Road
Mineral Point, WI 53565

To contact author: peaceisactive@gmail.com

ORDERING INFORMATION
Quantity sales. Special discounts are available on quantity purchases by corporations, associations, and others. For details, contact info@littlecreekpress.com

Orders by US trade bookstores and wholesalers.
Please contact Little Creek Press or Ingram for details.

Printed in the United States of America

Cataloging-in-Publication Data
Names: McCann, Tom, author
Title: Peace is Active
Description: Mineral Point, WI: Little Creek Press, 2023.
Identifiers: LCCN: 2022919853 | ISBN: 978-1-955656-38-2
Subjects: BIOGRAPHY & AUTOBIOGRAPHY / Social Activists

Book design by Mimi Bark and Little Creek Press

TABLE OF CONTENTS

CHAPTER 1

PEACEFUL PURPOSE

I was five years old when my friend ran away from my dad with a look of fear in his eyes I had never seen before.

My friend was a refugee from Laos named Kao. He was five years old, just like me. His family fled to the United States during the war in Vietnam and settled in my hometown of Eau Claire, Wisconsin.

I had no idea why he was afraid of my dad.

In addition to working as a custodian for the local school district, Dad was a soldier in the U.S. Army Reserves. He had military duties one weekend a month and two weeks each summer at Fort McCoy near Tomah, Wisconsin. Dad was one of the good guys. Fighting for liberty and justice for all. Defending America. Keeping us safe.

Dad would sometimes return home wearing his military uniform. Kao was afraid of soldiers. His family was forced to flee their home because the war in Vietnam was also fought in his country. To him, soldiers represented the violence his family was trying to avoid.

Dad was lucky. He was never sent to Vietnam. He was sent to South Korea to be a lifeguard at a swimming pool on a military base a few miles from the North Korean border. Many of his military friends were not so lucky. If Dad wasn't a lifeguard, he might have had a more dangerous assignment. He might have been killed. I think about that when I see lifeguards each summer.

Once I was old enough to understand what soldiers do, my pride for Dad was overshadowed by my worry for his safety. The threat of war was real. The United States was in a cold war with the Soviet Union, and tensions could boil into a hot war at any point. I spent some of my elementary school years hiding under my desk during nuclear bomb drills. I wasn't sure how my desk would save me from the thermal radiation of a nuclear blast.

War is a very dangerous place for civilians. Dads, moms, and kids often die or get seriously wounded. Families are forced to flee their homes. War is terrible. I felt really bad for Kao and other refugee families. I wanted to keep Dad safe, but I also wanted everyone else to be safe.

Growing up in a military family gave me purpose in life. Ever since I figured out what Dad was training for, peace on Earth has been my goal. I didn't want him to die in a war. I didn't want my family, or any other family, to suffer the brutalities of war. Living in peace is better than living in war. For everyone.

Now, here's the great news. Lots of people all over the world are working on the goal of peace. Many have been successful in numerous ways. We're getting better at doing business with each other instead of invading each other. For the first time in history, democratic republics are becoming the predominant form of government rather than dictatorships. Sometimes we take sad and stupid steps backward, but the steps forward have been far more plentiful for many generations.

Life on Earth is getting better. The technological and medical advances during the past few centuries have been incredible. More people have access to healthcare, education, and indoor plumbing than ever before. We have advanced tools to monitor air and water quality. We continue to make incredible advancements.

We're getting closer to achieving the goal of peace on Earth. We still have terrible outbreaks of violence, but the number of wars per decade has dropped rapidly over the past few centuries. We've never been closer to the goal of peace on Earth than now. A peaceful planet is the best strategy for all of us. We have the ability to live in peace.

Since Dad served in the military, I wanted huge peaceful steps forward as quickly as possible. I cheered for any politician, musician, or scientist dedicated to the goal of peace. Since the threat of war had scary consequences for my military family, I wanted to do something to help avoid wars.

History shows ordinary people often change the course of history. This is especially true in the digital age. Anyone from anywhere can say something or do something that ends up going viral. Millions of people can be reached quickly and cheaply. We communicate in ways that were not possible for prior generations. For many years, I had a poster in my bedroom with a quote from President John F. Kennedy that said, "It's time for a new generation of leadership. For there is a new world to be won."

We never know who will change the course of history. There are millions of scientists on this planet, but only a few of them will make life-changing discoveries. There are millions of leaders on this planet, but only a few of them will get elected and do great things. We need billions of people pursuing the goal of peace to increase the odds of success. If billions of us are pursuing peace, many of us will be in the right place at the right time to make a positive difference.

We all have the power to change the course of history. We all make decisions that influence the future such as who we vote for, what we purchase, how we spend our time, and how we treat others. These things all affect the future.

Sometimes, the course of history is changed in unexpected ways. We might help a random stranger who goes on to make a great discovery. We might donate money to a refugee charity that helps a young woman become a peaceful world leader. We don't always know how our actions will influence the course of history.

On the other hand, sometimes we know exactly how our actions influence the future. We live longer if we eat healthier. We feel better if we get enough sleep. We breathe easier if we limit air pollution. These are all decisions we have the power to make.

Since I grew up in a military family, I became one of the billions of people on Earth wanting to create a more peaceful future. Maybe I could help in some way. Perhaps I would be in the right place at the right time. Maybe I would do a good deed that ripples throughout history in unexpected ways. Maybe I would somehow stop a war before it begins. I wasn't sure what I would do, but Dad was training for war. Peace on Earth was my goal.

My mom took my two brothers and me to church every Sunday so my first thought was to promote peace as a religious leader. I remember seeing clips of Martin Luther King, Jr. showing how inspirational he was. I wanted to get married and have a family so being a Catholic priest wasn't the best option for me.

I've always enjoyed music. I thought about writing songs to encourage global harmony. I heard John Lennon singing about giving peace a chance. I sang in school choirs growing up. I even sang inside Westminster Abbey in London during a high school choir trip. The experience of hearing our voices reverberating off the high cathedral ceiling made me realize how powerful and inspirational music can be. Maybe I could make a difference with music.

I had a lot of great teachers. They taught me to focus on the facts and always be open to new ideas. My mom was a first-grade teacher, and I was always proud of her for that. Maybe I could teach and motivate students to create a peaceful future.

My parents and I often watched the nightly news. I saw talented journalists sharing stories from all over the world. I wanted everyone to know what was going on in the world. I started thinking about being a journalist.

Then I saw democratic leaders changing the course of history by winning elections. I saw progress on peace deals, human rights, and clean water rules. Being a priest, musician, teacher, or journalist might allow me to influence other people, but the democratic process seemed like the best way to make a real difference in the world. The democratic process can lead to millions of people being lifted out of poverty, getting access to healthcare, and living peaceful lives by electing peaceful leaders instead of warmongers.

My original goal of stopping wars to save Dad was a nearly impossible goal to set for myself. If Dad died in a war, it would be ridiculous to blame myself. I decided I would be proud of myself as long as I tried to make the world more peaceful in whatever way I could. I had no idea the goal of peace would send me on a lifelong journey to the center of the 2020 presidential election.

CHAPTER 2

OLD ABE

Making a difference in the world seemed impossible for someone like me from northern Wisconsin. Then again, I grew up hearing stories about how my family played a role in the history of the United States. My family's most famous "difference maker" was a pet eagle.

My great-great-grandparents traded corn with members of the Ojibwe tribe to adopt a young eaglet near their home in Jim Falls, Wisconsin. They put their children in charge of trapping mice to feed the eaglet. They had no idea the little eaglet would grow up to be famous.

My great-great-grandfather, Dan McCann, migrated to Wisconsin from Ohio to work in the northern Wisconsin timber industry. My great-great-grandmother, Margaretta McCann, migrated with her family to Prairie du Chien, Wisconsin. She is the reason I grew up being told I was part Native American.

I'm not sure if Native "American" is the right phrase since the Anishinaabe tribes migrated to the Great Lakes area generations before the name America was used. A European merchant named Amerigo Vespucci wrote two widely read pamphlets in 1503 and 1505 about new lands being explored. Mapmakers needed a name for the lands Amerigo wrote about, so they used the Latinized version of his name, America.

I'm not sure if "native" is the right word, either. Some of my ancestors were just the first people to arrive. The Anishinaabe tribes migrated to the Great Lakes area from what is now called California because they heard wild rice grew on the water. During the agricultural revolution, European farmers migrated to Wisconsin to grow crops. During the industrial revolution, people migrated to Wisconsin to work in factories along the shores of Lake Michigan. We all come from immigrant families.

It would be great if different groups of people could solve their differences without wars, but that wasn't the case during the American Civil War from 1861 to 1865. It was a war with enough bullets and cannonballs to rip dads and brothers apart but not enough medical advances to put them back together.

When soldiers were leaving northern Wisconsin to fight in the Civil War, my great-great-grandfather sold the pet eagle to the troops heading to Madison for military training at Camp Randall. After buying their eagle mascot, the troops decided to call themselves the Eau Claire Eagles. They named the eagle Old Abe in honor of President Abraham Lincoln.

Old Abe arrived at Camp Randall screeching and squawking. Old Abe was often perched on a wooden stand carried by the soldiers from Eau Claire. When the eagle would screech, the soldiers would cheer. Old Abe encouraged the home team at Camp Randall by jumping around, just like Badger football fans would jump around Camp Randall Stadium generations later.

Old Abe became famous in the Civil War for motivating troops in over thirty battles. There were reports of Confederate generals offering rewards for anyone who could "kill that Yankee buzzard!" After the war, the story of Old Abe was told in newspapers across the country. Old Abe continued as a military mascot and was featured at rallies and parades for many years.

After the death of Old Abe, the eagle was preserved and put on display at the Wisconsin State Capitol. Eau Claire Memorial High School has an Old Abe eagle mascot. Soldiers from one of the most storied military divisions in the United States Army, the 101st Airborne Division, are known as the Screaming Eagles, with a patch on their shoulders emblazoned with an image of Old Abe.

Old Abe set a high bar in terms of making a difference. My great-great-grandparents' pet eagle was in the right place at the right time. If a pet eagle could influence the course of history, anything is possible. I wasn't sure how I would make a difference in the world, but I was going to try.

CHAPTER 3

GOVERNOR TOMMY THOMPSON

In 1991, Wisconsin Governor Tommy Thompson held a press conference at my high school. I wasn't a journalist, but I had a few questions I wanted to ask him. I grabbed a notepad and walked right up to the governor in a hallway where reporters were asking him questions. I asked him what he planned to do about the jobs lost at the local tire factory. He gave me an answer that mostly avoided the question.

The next day, the front page of the school newspaper included a picture of me asking the governor my question. The picture made me look like a journalist holding a notepad and pen. That picture made me think about my future again. Maybe being a journalist was the answer to how I would make a difference in the world. I would rather be a journalist asking good questions than a politician avoiding questions.

People often ask kids what they want to be when they grow up, and most kids don't know what to say. I tried telling people I wanted to stop wars and make the world a more peaceful place, but most people gave me odd looks. Some people asked how I would support myself while not having a real job.

I started to think about what my real job would be. I could make the world better by being a teacher, journalist, scientist, elected leader, etc., but getting those jobs wasn't easy. My grandpa owned a windows and awnings business, and I often saw the sales and installation process while helping him. I began thinking about starting my own business. I thought about selling solar panels to help make the world a better place.

During my junior year of high school, I joined a sales and marketing club called the Distributive Education Clubs of America, but everyone just called it DECA. I wanted to attend the DECA state convention in Madison, but I needed to win a regional sales and marketing competition. Another option for attending the state convention was to launch a campaign to be one of the regional DECA state vice presidents. I wasn't sure if I could win a sales and marketing competition, but to be on the election ballot, all I had to do was submit my name.

It was my first campaign. One of my teachers drove me to the state convention in Madison. I enjoyed meeting students from other high schools. I had no idea what I was getting into when I won the election. A few weeks later, I was told the funding for our student organization was being cut.

It wasn't just DECA funding being cut. Wisconsin politicians were trying to cut many student organizations such as Future Farmers of America (FFA), Future Business Leaders of America (FBLA), and many others. It seemed obvious that student organizations should be expanded, not cut.

Wisconsin Democratic State Assembly Representative Barbara

Gronemus opposed the funding cuts. She asked the elected leaders of the student organizations to come to the state capitol in Madison. We headed to Madison to meet with politicians. Our goal was to explain how student organizations benefit the state of Wisconsin.

Some politicians asked why we should educate Wisconsin kids when the most educated students often leave the state after graduating. We reminded them that most Wisconsin doctors, engineers, and farmers grew up in Wisconsin and attended Wisconsin schools. I don't remember what one of the scarier politicians asked us, but I remember being nervous before meeting someone named Snarlin' Marlin Schneider.

What happened next was an emotional whiplash. The funding for student organizations was added back to the budget. We were thrilled with our victory. Then Governor Tommy Thompson cut the funding with his veto pen. We were devastated. We thought we had secured education funding for thousands of students across the state, but the funding was cut.

Most of the politicians and teachers told us we did a great job, but they said the fight was over. We lost. We asked if we could get enough votes to override the governor's veto. We were told Governor Thompson had never had a veto overridden before, so it was highly unlikely.

We didn't care how unlikely it was. Fighting for education was the right thing to do, and we were going to keep doing it. We wrote letters to the editor in newspapers all over Wisconsin. We asked high school students to contact their local politicians and tell them how important student organizations are.

A few weeks later, we got a call from Representative Gronemus saying we had enough votes to override the governor's veto. The next call came from someone in the governor's office offering to fund the organizations without holding the vote to override the veto.

We wanted to hold the vote. We wanted everyone to know a bunch of students had the power to override the governor. However, the student organization funding was the main goal, so we happily accepted the deal from the governor's office.

When I joined DECA, I didn't know I would end up being part of a student movement that secured education funding for thousands of students across the state. I just wanted to learn how to start my own business.

Helping secure education funding gave me confidence that my decisions and actions could influence the future. I happened to be in the right place at the right time. I wanted to continue finding ways to make a difference.

Since I witnessed the power young people could have on the political process, I tried to motivate more students to get involved. I created the Youth Organization for Us (YOU) and started recruiting members. I tried to make the organization as nonpartisan as possible with the simple goal of getting young people involved in their communities.

Was the youth organization successful? No, but I learned important lessons that would help me with future projects. Legendary Green Bay Packers coach Vince Lombardi once said, "It's not whether you get knocked down, it's whether you get back up."

CHAPTER 4

LOS ANGELES, CALIFORNIA

In April 1992, a few months before graduating high school, I attended the national DECA convention in Los Angeles, California. My older brother was a full-time soldier stationed at Fort Ord near Monterey, California. He drove down to visit me while I was in Los Angeles. I had no idea we were about to find ourselves in the middle of the Los Angeles riots.

About two months before the DECA convention, a video was released of a 25 year old Black man, Rodney King, being beaten by multiple White police officers. The police officers were taken to court and faced long prison sentences if found guilty. The entire Los Angeles community was on edge as they waited to hear the verdict. The day after I arrived in Los Angeles for the DECA convention, the court announced there would be no prison time for the police officers. This news created an explosion of anger and sadness that swept the city of Los Angeles for the next six days.

The first thing on the national DECA convention schedule was a trip to Disneyland. The amusement park was open but mostly empty due to the riots. There were no lines as we enjoyed one of the best days of our lives. It didn't dawn on us how privileged we were to have such a great day as the city around us was hurting and burning.

The next day, I was excited to go to a baseball game at Dodger Stadium with my older brother. We grew up playing baseball. We spent hours listening to legendary baseball announcer Bob Uecker tell jokes and stories during Milwaukee Brewers games. My brother picked me up in his truck, and we headed to Dodger Stadium.

Since this was 1992, we didn't have digital maps or instant access to news. People were starting to use mobile phones, but neither of us had one. We knew there had been riots after the Rodney King verdict the night before, but we thought the riots were over. As we got closer to the stadium, we got off the main highway. We noticed metal gates had been pulled down over many restaurant and storefront windows. It was mostly Korean restaurants. We started to see some damage from the night before.

We didn't know what was going on. We didn't realize there had been a conflict brewing between the Black and Korean communities in Los Angeles for many years. Koreans moved to Los Angeles in large numbers in the 1960s after the Korean War. They started buying lots of businesses and restaurants in Los Angeles which included a lot of businesses in predominantly Black neighborhoods.

There are lots of reasons why people don't get along. In some cases, there are misunderstood cultural differences. In Korean culture, looking someone in the eye is not respectful. For many Black residents making purchases at Korean businesses, the lack of eye contact was seen as a sign of disrespect. Many people got to know each other and became friends, but the language and cultural barriers created tension.

In addition to cultural differences, there had been an incident where a Korean business owner shot a young girl during a shoplifting incident. After the Rodney King verdict was announced, the Black community expressed their anger and frustrations in many ways, including attacks on Korean businesses, especially in the Koreatown area on our way to Dodger Stadium.

We weren't sure what to do, so we continued driving to Dodger Stadium, thinking it would be the safest place. A wave of panic came over me when we realized the gates of Dodger Stadium were locked and the game had been canceled.

We didn't want to go back to the hotel the same way we had come. We started driving away from Dodger Stadium and noticed columns of smoke rising on the horizon. The smoke was actually helpful since it told us to go in the opposite direction. As we were driving, we saw a green military helicopter buzz over us really fast and low with what looked like missiles attached to the bottom. The only other time I had seen a military helicopter like that was in war movies. My brother sat up straight, got an intense look on his face, and said, "We need to get on a major highway as quickly as possible."

We made it safely to the highway and back to the hotel. I felt a huge sense of relief to be back at the hotel. News coverage showed damage impacting many areas, especially in Koreatown, where we had been. From my window near the top of the hotel, I spent the rest of my trip watching a sad number of smoke columns rising from the Los Angeles horizon.

Over sixty people were killed. More than two thousand people were injured. The Los Angeles Police Department arrested over twelve thousand people with the help of the United States Military and the

California National Guard. That drive through Koreatown felt like a war zone because, on that day, it was.

As I thought about my brother driving back to his military base, I was more determined than ever to pursue the goal of peace. Having one of the best days of my life at Disneyland and one of the scariest days of my life back-to-back was a huge reality check. After my experiences during the Los Angeles riots, I was determined to make the world a better place. After high school, I wanted to go to college to learn how to do it.

Studying at a good college meant loans, scholarships, or spending some time in the military first. I spent my high school years trying to win scholarships so I could afford to go to college. I wasn't great at standardized tests, but I was willing to work hard to get good grades. In addition to my schoolwork, I joined every club and ran for every leadership position available so that I could list them on my college applications. I remember a teacher warning me I would have gray hair before I left high school if I kept doing so many things.

As a high school junior, I was upset with Wisconsin Governor Tommy Thompson for trying to cut student organization funding. However, as a high school senior, I was thankful Governor Thompson had created a scholarship program with the top students from each Wisconsin high school receiving a full academic scholarship to the University of Wisconsin.

I felt fortunate, relieved, and exhausted when the academic scholarship was awarded to me at the end of my senior year of high school. It was an incredible opportunity to study at the University of Wisconsin. I wanted to learn why wars happen and how to stop them before they begin. I remember thinking I was now indebted to the taxpayers of

Wisconsin for funding my scholarship. I intended to pay them back by helping to create a more peaceful world for all of us.

UW-Madison was a great place to go to school. I enjoyed meeting people from all over the world. Since my hometown in northern Wisconsin was roughly ninety-five percent White, this was a new experience for me. Other cultures can be very different, but I soon realized we're all the same in many ways. A classmate of mine was from Russia. He laughed when we started getting to know each other. He said we didn't have to be Cold War enemies anymore because we were both Wisconsin Badgers now. Imagine if everyone on the planet realized we're all on the same team now.

I studied political science and history in college. I wanted to find the lessons from past wars to help avoid future wars. I confirmed a very obvious lesson: Wars are terrible, brutal, tragic, and stupid. On the bright side, I also found a long history of people actively pursuing the goal of peace with incredible stories of success.

Studying war and peace made me nervous for my military family. Dad retired from the U.S. Army Reserves, but my older brother was in the U.S. Army as a full-time soldier. The threat of war was still very real for my family. I had no idea what I would do, but I wanted to make the world a more peaceful place in any way I could.

CHAPTER 5

U.S. SENATOR TAMMY BALDWIN

I was a junior at UW-Madison when a very rude Republican ran against future U.S. Senator Tammy Baldwin in the state assembly district where I lived on campus. The Republican attacked her sexual identity with crass comments. I grew up in a fairly conservative home and considered myself a moderate, but there was no way I was voting for this Republican.

The state assembly district in Madison was, and still is, heavily liberal, with no Republican ever winning more than thirty-five percent of the vote. Tammy Baldwin easily defeated her opponent, but I didn't like that someone could run a campaign just to have a platform to say terrible things.

I wondered if the same Republican would run against Tammy Baldwin in the next election two years later. I hoped he would not. I started to think if the same guy ran on the Republican side, I would run against him and try to defeat him in the Republican primary.

Two years later, in 1996, I had just graduated from college and decided to stay in Madison to wait for my girlfriend (now wife and mother of our two wonderful children) to graduate. I found a one-year job managing a student dormitory. I worked during business hours and was mostly free on nights and weekends. Since I had time on my hands, I started seriously thinking about running for state assembly.

Trying to win a primary election would be real-world campaign experience for a political science graduate like myself. I considered the campaign my senior year project even though I had already graduated. I wasn't sure where my girlfriend and I would find jobs after she graduated, but there was no way I would win the general election running as a Republican in an overwhelmingly liberal district. It was a perfect opportunity to gain experience running a political campaign with no chance of a long-term commitment.

I started to think about how to win the Republican primary. I sent a press release to reporters announcing I was running for state assembly, hoping the prior Republican candidate would see the news and decide not to run. I'm not sure if my plan worked or if the guy had no plans to run anyway, but the candidate deadline passed, and I was the only Republican running against Tammy Baldwin.

I set a new goal after finding out there would be no primary election. I wanted to get as much campaign experience as possible while heading toward an honorable defeat in a district no Republican had ever won.

Fundraising was much easier than I thought it would be. The state of Wisconsin would give me matching campaign funds for the first few thousand dollars I raised. I figured out where wealthy Republican neighborhoods were and went door to door, saying I was the Republican candidate running against Tammy Baldwin. I easily raised enough money to get the matching campaign funds. I made a budget and started buying signs and advertisements.

To reach people off campus, I put an insert in the weekend newspaper for the zip codes in my district. The insert explained I was a moderate candidate supporting more funding for education. I bought some yard signs and felt excited to see them spring up around the city.

I noticed most of the student newspapers on campus were left on desks with the paper creased to show the crossword puzzle. There were no ads around the crossword puzzle, but I asked the student newspaper if they would allow me to sponsor the crossword puzzle. Lots of people told me it was a great idea when they started seeing my campaign ads in classes all over campus.

Signs and newspaper advertisements brought attention to my campaign, but I needed to speak directly with voters. I found a map showing Madison city streets in my district and started crossing them off as I knocked on the door of each house. I had a lot of great conversations, even though most people said they would never vote for a Republican.

The local newspaper contacted me to schedule an interview with a writer named John Nichols. He was very nice and surprised me with his casual clothes, sandals, and laid-back office space. I was expecting the suits and ties I had seen in the movies. John asked me questions about my campaign and then wrote a great story with the headline, "Republican Candidate Supports ... Clinton." The article told my story of being a moderate candidate in a very liberal district.

The newspaper story led to more people knowing who I was. I scheduled meetings with student organizations and continued my attempt to knock on every door in the district. One day, I saw a woman point to one of my campaign signs as she said to another woman, "That's who I'm voting for." That motivated me to keep knocking on more doors.

A few weeks later, Tammy Baldwin easily won the election. I was proud of my campaign. It was worth the time and effort. I met a lot of great people, learned many lessons about campaigns, and got to see my name on the 1996 presidential ballot. I didn't have the opportunity to defeat the prior Republican candidate in the primary, but it felt good knowing I was ready to defeat him if he had run.

Even though I ran in a district I had no chance of winning, the experience of running a campaign taught me multiple lessons. Running a campaign is difficult work and costs a lot of money. The operational aspects of a campaign are almost as important as the message being delivered. One person can't do everything. You need to raise a lot of money to hire a lot of people. You need to find volunteers willing to spend hours devoted to campaign efforts. The end of my campaign for state assembly was the beginning of what would be a lifelong respect for candidates, campaign workers, and volunteers.

Two years later, in 1998, Tammy Baldwin was elected to the U.S. House of Representatives. She was then elected to the U.S. Senate in 2012. I have always admired her. She runs positive campaigns and focuses on issues important to the people she represents.

It was unlikely that Senator Baldwin would become a U.S. senator. There were very few women, especially women who were not wealthy, in the U.S. Senate. Tammy Baldwin wanted to make a difference in the world. The odds were against her, but she became a senator. There are many stories similar to this where unlikely people end up being a part of history.

The founder of Earth Day grew up in northern Wisconsin, surrounded by corn fields, cows, and lakes. Gaylord Nelson left Wisconsin to fight on the Japanese island of Okinawa during World War II. When he returned, he entered politics, was elected Wisconsin governor, and later to the U.S. Senate. He was an environmentalist and strongly opposed the war in Vietnam. Earth Day is celebrated all over the world on April 22. None of this would have happened if he had been killed while serving in the military.

Vel Phillips from Milwaukee, Wisconsin, was the first Black woman to graduate from the University of Wisconsin Law School. She was the first female judge in Milwaukee County. She was then elected to be Wisconsin's secretary of state. In the 1950s, nobody would have bet on a young Black woman in Milwaukee to become so successful and influential.

We need lots of people dedicated to making the world a better place. We never know who will be in the right place at the right time to make a difference. Some people will become political leaders, musicians, or popular athletes with platforms to influence the course of history. Most of us will be normal people making the world a better place in our own unique ways.

CHAPTER 6

10,000 FEET ABOVE 9/11

After the state assembly campaign, my girlfriend and I got jobs in the suburbs of Minneapolis, Minnesota. She worked for a consulting company, and I was working for a small technology company in Burnsville, Minnesota. I was calling large corporations and universities to sell network attachable storage devices.

I enjoyed working in sales because it was a fun game to play with automatic commission pay raises if I did a good job. I was one of the top salespeople at the company. We were living in a nice apartment and bought a car. I had a real job!

I was still focused on making the world a better place in my free time. I was checking out bags of books from the library each week. I started learning the things they don't teach in schools. I studied history in college and learned a lot, but I didn't see the larger picture until I read books such as *A People's History of the United States* by Howard Zinn. I studied international relations but didn't see the full global chess board until I started doing my own research.

I didn't mind the sales and marketing job at the small tech company in Minnesota, but I wanted to find a way to work on the goal of peace full-time. I was still thinking about starting my own business to sell solar panels. It would be a great way to make a difference while generating income.

One day at my sales job, I was told I didn't get a commission because one of my large accounts made their purchase through the new company website. That was a huge red flag to me. My first thought was websites would soon replace salespeople. I needed to find a different line of work, or I needed to be the owner of the website.

The next time I went to the library, I checked out books to teach myself how to build websites. After a couple of months of learning the basics, I bought a software program that made building websites fairly easy. I decided I would start building an online sales and marketing company.

My first website was dedicated to making the world a better place. I wrote a book about peace and created a website to post the book online for anyone to read. It was fun checking how many people visited the site each day. I enjoyed reading comments from all over the world.

The internet had not been around very long when I started building websites in 1998, but the internet stock market boom was just taking off. It felt like the opening of a completely new market full of opportunities. I liked the idea of websites making money for me while I was sleeping, eating, and trying to make the world more peaceful.

My goal was automated mobile income. If I could generate online revenue in automated ways, my wife and I (we got married shortly after college in 1998) would be free to live anywhere we wanted. Other than updating the websites, we would have time to follow our interests and passions. I thought it sounded like a dream, but there were plenty of stories about people making it work.

I left my sales and marketing job and started building websites full-time. Before having children, we moved to Colorado to enjoy the mountains for a few years. We lived in an apartment just north of Denver and started looking for a house to buy.

One night, I watched a news segment about urban sprawl in Atlanta, Georgia. I told myself I would never want to live in a place like that! Then they cut to the second largest example of urban sprawl: the suburbs of Denver, Colorado, where our apartment was. Yikes! We stopped looking for a home to buy in the suburbs and started looking in the mountains.

Most of the mountain homes were too expensive for us, but we noticed the prices were lower the higher up the mountains we went. We found an affordable home at 10,000 feet above sea level near St. Mary's Glacier, about twenty minutes from an old mining town called Idaho Springs, Colorado. We saw the house and bought it during a beautiful Rocky Mountain summer. The challenges posed by mountain winters at this elevation were not apparent to us at the time.

A month later, we drove a rental truck from our apartment north of Denver to our new home way, way up in the mountains. It took most of the day to pack the truck, so we started our drive into the mountains later in the day. By the time we reached our new home, the sun was dipping below the mountain peaks and the air was getting chilly. Then it began to snow.

Our plan was to move a few things into the house right away but leave most of the unloading for the following day. I was opening the back of the truck when my wife walked up to me with a worried look on her face. She said the house door had shut and was now locked with the key inside. After checking all the other doors and windows, we realized we were locked out of the house with temperatures dropping and snow accumulating.

We thought about sleeping in the truck, but we might not have enough gas to keep us warm. We thought about driving the truck back down the mountain to stay in a hotel, but heavy snow was falling, which meant the mountain roads were slippery. Within the first few minutes of arriving at our mountain home, we already faced a difficult situation.

I started thinking about how to break into my new home. I walked around the house and decided breaking a window would be the worst option. There was a door to the house in the garage that would be protected from the cold, so I decided my best option was to break down that internal door. Luckily, the doorframe was old, and it broke the second time I kicked it. We were safely inside the house. I hugged my wife as we laughed about putting "fix the door" on our first house project list.

Once we moved the rest of our items into the house the following day, I set up my computer and connected to the internet. Only one phone line strung along the mountain roads served our small neighborhood. Heavy snow, wind, and falling trees made the phone line an unreliable connection to the rest of the world, but as long as the phone line was working, I would be able to create websites and connect with people anywhere on the planet.

I wasn't sure what I would sell with my websites, but I learned about a new thing called affiliate marketing. I would be paid a commission if someone clicked a link on my website and bought something. Most of the big-name brands had affiliate marketing programs. I was able to sell items and make a commission without producing, buying, storing, or shipping anything.

I created an online shopping mall to sell everything. It was a directory of online stores. I applied to every affiliate program I could find and added each one to my new online shopping mall. I started generating commissions with direct deposits flowing into my business bank account. This was so amazing! Did I actually find an automated way to make money that would allow me to spend the rest of my life trying to make the world a more peaceful place?

I set up my computer to *ding* whenever there was a sale. One day, the computer started dinging a lot. A section of my online mall promoted a well-known underwear company. One of my website's pages was now listed as the top option on Google when people searched for a specific type of men's underwear. People would visit my website and then quickly click the link to the well-known underwear website. Lots of underwear was purchased, and my commissions were rising quickly. Being ranked on top of the first page of Google search results for popular shopping keywords is like winning the Google lottery.

My wife asked me where the money was coming from. I told her I somehow became one of the top underwear sellers on the internet. We both laughed about the odd course life can take. There was never a moment in my life when I thought I would grow up to be an underwear salesman, but here I was.

The underwear sales were great for about a month. Then Google changed the algorithm that generates their search listings. My underwear shopping page dropped from the first listing on the first page to the middle of the third page. Sales dropped to zero. Online salespeople call this the "Google Slap" that knocks your website down the listings while slapping you back to reality. The online sales and marketing game was fun, but it was a tough, competitive game with constant changes.

Since generating free traffic from Google was difficult, I started buying ads on Google searches. I bought ads that were shown in wealthy zip codes leading to my affiliate links for jewelry stores, travel agencies, and online art galleries. I felt like Robinhood trying to get money from rich people so I could spend my time trying to improve the world.

Travel packages became my top income generator. I decided to build a travel website focused on selling all-inclusive resort packages (even though I had never been to an all-inclusive resort.) I made a page for each resort with details, pictures, and an affiliate sales link. I dreamed of sitting in the shade on a tropical beach, watching my internet income grow while writing a book about world peace. I had some success with travel websites, but the income wasn't reliable enough to support us.

I wasn't the only person struggling to make money on the internet. At the turn of the century, the internet boom turned into an internet bust. Some people called it the "dot-com crash." Lots of people lost money and jobs. My wife lost her software consulting job. We were now living in a rural mountain top community with a house payment due, and no steady income or health insurance.

The only jobs we could find were in the mountain community of Georgetown, Colorado, about a half-hour drive from our house. My wife was guiding tour groups at an old silver mine, and I was working at a home for boys who were court-ordered to be there. Both of us were making less combined than she used to make at her software consulting job.

I was a counselor for the eight boys who lived in the home where I worked. I woke them up each weekday and helped them prepare breakfast before school. It was my job to ensure the kids were respectful to the teachers and therapists who came to the house each day. I would help make lunch and fill out reports. I really enjoyed taking the kids to play football and basketball at a local park during their breaks.

The young boys were known as juvenile delinquents, but they were not bad kids. Most of them came from dysfunctional families and often lived in impoverished conditions. One of the younger boys was at the juvenile home because he was caught selling marijuana. He told me he sold marijuana to buy food since his homeless family lived out of a car. Another kid was from Columbine High School near Denver, where many students had recently been killed during a school shooting. I felt bad for these kids and did everything I could to respect and help them.

I enjoyed making a difference in the lives of the kids I worked with. My wife and I weren't making much money, but it was enough to pay the bills. Maybe this is what I would do for the rest of my life. I really enjoyed living in the mountains. We didn't go to expensive ski resorts but enjoyed hiking beautiful trails throughout the Rocky Mountains. Life was good, especially compared to the lives of the kids I worked with.

The kids at the juvenile home ate breakfast each morning at a big table in the main room of the house. An old square television was mounted near the ceiling in one of the corners. We enjoyed watching cartoons on public television as we ate breakfast. One day, the kids were flipping through the channels when I saw smoke coming out of a skyscraper. I asked them to go back to the channel to see what was happening. It was Tuesday morning, September 11, 2001.

I was shocked to see two airplanes had crashed into the World Trade Center skyscrapers in New York City. People thought it was an accident after the first crash, but a different plane hitting the second tower made it obvious this was a terrorist attack.

We watched the news coverage for most of the day. Some of the kids were excited by the thought of going to war against whoever did this. One of the maintenance workers was already expressing anti-Muslim rhetoric. I was saddened by the news of thousands of people being killed. I was worried about the future. My brother spent three years as a full-time soldier, but he was now going to college with the money he earned by serving in the military. There wasn't an immediate threat to my family, but there was an immediate threat to the country and to the goal of peace.

Most peace activists are automatically considered pacifists who oppose all wars in all situations. That is not the case for me. I was proud of my grandparents for fighting the German Nazi army during World War II, as the Nazis stole land, resources, and millions of lives. We need to be active for peace to avoid wars, but we must also defend ourselves and defeat war criminals to achieve peace.

When people hijack airplanes and crash them into civilian-filled skyscrapers, there is no doubt we need to defend ourselves. The only question is how to defend ourselves. Would wars keep us safe, or would they worsen the problem by leading to more violent actions?

Who would we go to war against? The hijackers were discovered to be a terrorist group called al-Qaeda, led by a man named Osama bin Laden. Most of the people involved in the 9/11 attacks were from Saudi Arabia. They were mad at the United States for supporting the dictatorship that ruled Saudi Arabia. They were also mad because the United States had used Saudi Arabia as a military staging area during a recent war in Iraq and Kuwait.

I started researching the history of Saudi Arabia and other countries in the region to figure out why we were attacked and what we could do to stop future attacks. Most people in the United States didn't want to wait until we had a clear picture of what had happened. Our country was attacked, and someone needed to pay the price. We needed to show the world it was a mistake to attack the United States of America. The nation was hungry for revenge.

My research led to a lot of information not included in the nightly newscasts. It turns out the United States used to support Osama bin Laden and other religious extremists like him. During the Cold War with the Soviet Union, we helped "freedom fighters" like Osama bin Laden fight against Soviet troops in Afghanistan.

Some American funding in Afghanistan supported religious schools that taught children to kill all infidels in a global holy war. Some American funding was used to deliver American-made Stinger missiles to help shoot down Soviet helicopters. After the Soviet Union lost their war in Afghanistan, American intelligence agencies mostly forgot about the religious militants we helped fund and train until they attacked us on September 11, 2001.

After 9/11, I thought it made sense for the U.S. military to attack the al-Qaeda terrorist training camps in Afghanistan. There was an immediate need to disrupt the planning and training for future attacks. We also needed to show there was no place to hide if you attacked the United States.

In addition to striking the al-Qaeda camps, President George W. Bush started talking about overthrowing Afghanistan's government to punish them for hosting the al-Qaeda terrorist camps. This would require the U.S. military to invade and occupy the entire country of Afghanistan, leading to a much larger war.

I didn't think occupying all of Afghanistan was a good idea. We would mainly be fighting against the Pashtun people who lived in southeast Afghanistan and across the border in Pakistan. Would we extend the war into Pakistan or let the Pashtun fighters have a sanctuary in Pakistan as we fought them in Afghanistan? Nothing about occupying Afghanistan made sense to me. I decided it was a war I needed to stop. I no longer had family members in the military, but this would be a very costly occupation that needed to be stopped.

CHAPTER 7

COSTLY WARS

Five months after the September 11 attacks, U.S. President George W. Bush gave a speech declaring there was an "axis of evil" with the countries of Iraq, Iran, and North Korea threatening us. This made no sense to me at all. None of those countries had anything to do with the attacks on 9/11, and none were allied with each other.

President Bush said we needed to invade and occupy Iraq. Really? At the same time we were trying to occupy Afghanistan? That was when I realized the Bush administration was intentionally misleading the American people. They were using the fear caused by the attacks on 9/11 to mislead the United States into a war with Iraq.

The Bush administration was full of former oil company executives and imperialists who wanted to use American military power to conquer distant lands and resources. Before George W. Bush was elected, many of his supporters were part of an organization called Project for the New American Century. They used the organization to promote a war with Iraq. Most of the people from the organization ended up being senior-level officials in the Bush administration. Billions of dollars in oil contracts would be opened up by overthrowing the governments in Iraq and Iran. After the attacks on 9/11, they saw an opening to pursue their corrupt plans. All they had to do was shift attention from Afghanistan to Iraq.

I wasn't sure why the Bush administration wanted to occupy all of Afghanistan, but after they declared war on Iraq, their plan came into focus for me. If the goal of the Bush administration was to invade and occupy Iraq and Iran, then having large military bases in Afghanistan on Iran's eastern border would help create a two-front war on Iran after the occupation of Iraq was declared mission accomplished.

To generate support for a war in Iraq, the Bush administration claimed we would be greeted as liberators. This gave people the impression the war would be easy. The Bush administration left out the part where the Kurdish population in northern Iraq and the Shia population in southern Iraq might greet us as liberators, but the Sunni population in central Iraq would definitely not welcome us. Most Americans didn't know the difference between the Kurds, Shia, and Sunni in Iraq, but anyone who knew the difference knew the Bush administration was intentionally misleading people about American soldiers being greeted as liberators.

Republicans found it very easy to switch the attention from the war in Afghanistan to their desired war in Iraq. People in the United States were scared after the attacks on 9/11 and were more scared when the Bush administration claimed weapons in Iraq might lead to a "mushroom cloud" destroying an American city. The Bush administration used the threat of nuclear bombs and chemical weapons to scare people into supporting the invasion and occupation of Iraq.

There were no nuclear weapons found in Iraq. The weapons of mass destruction found by the inspectors were old chemical weapons the United States helped Iraq acquire during the Iraq-Iran War in the 1980s. When I found out we used to support the leader of Iraq, Saddam Hussein, in a prior war, it reminded me we had also supported Osama bin Laden in Afghanistan. If these people are so evil that we must now send our loved ones to fight them, why did we give both of them money and weapons a few years earlier?

The questions I asked were not the same ones the media asked. Most of the news coverage was in favor of the wars. In the months before the war in Iraq, a small percentage of the newscasts included voices that opposed the war. No media company wanted to risk its advertising profits by opposing the national march to war. We even started singing "God Bless America" at baseball games to add a little religious nationalism to the war campaign. You could almost hear the war drums beating as the country was patriotically misled into a costly war in Iraq.

Once war fever hits a population, it is really tough to stop it. Support for war is often an emotional response. It includes feelings of fear, disrespect, revenge, patriotism, and strength. It takes a lot of courage to say the opposite of what everyone else is saying. Even though I, and many others, were trying to oppose the occupations of Afghanistan and Iraq, nobody was listening. The banging of the war drums from the media and the Bush administration was too loud. I felt powerless to stop the wars.

I remembered what it felt like to be on the pro-war side. I cheered for the United States a decade earlier when we kicked Iraqi troops out of Kuwait. I was in high school and stayed home to watch the start of the war on the recently created twenty-four-hour news channel, CNN. They had reporters and cameras in Iraq capturing incredible footage. I saw tracer fire from Iraqi weapons trying to shoot down American pilots as the Americans bombed buildings in Iraq's capital, Baghdad, and other areas.

It was easy to get caught up in the patriotic mood of the country. It was easy to cheer for the home team. Watching the war on CNN was like watching a video game. We never saw the realities of war. It looked like a fireworks display we could safely watch from a distance.

I wanted America to win. I didn't know anything about Iraq. I just knew what the map looked like as the coach of Team USA, General Stormin' Norman Schwarzkopf, showed us how he called an end around play with troops pretending to go one way and then quickly advancing around the bend of the map to score a touchdown. I mean win the war. It was fun cheering for the home team.

It was a huge shift from being such a cheerleader during the first war in Iraq to doing everything I could to stop the second war in Iraq. Lots of people told me I was a traitor for opposing the war. I told people I was supporting the troops by opposing oil company warmongers who were misleading our military into a brutal and costly war. People laughed at me and said we would easily win the war within a few weeks.

Unfortunately, most of us know how the story ends. The U.S. military was powerful enough to occupy Afghanistan and Iraq, but we never got the support of the local populations. After early military victories, the United States was bogged down in costly guerilla warfare in Iraq and Afghanistan for many years. The civilian deaths in Iraq and Afghanistan were far greater than the number of soldiers killed and wounded.

The failed wars in Iraq and Afghanistan convinced me to get more involved in politics. I saw how easy it was for a bunch of oil executives to "patriotically" march us into costly wars. I saw millions of people rally around the flag when oil executives lied about mushroom clouds destroying American cities.

Who we elect to power makes a big difference. I decided to get more involved in the democratic process to stop these costly wars. Stopping wars is very difficult, but stopping warmongers from being elected to office is an achievable goal.

CHAPTER 8

POLITICAL CORRUPTION

I'm fortunate to live in a constitutional democratic republic. I have the freedom to get involved with the political process. It is very different for people who live under dictatorships. Peace activists are often imprisoned for protesting wars. Access to information is restricted or heavily scripted. Secret police threaten to kill people for being active for peace. With democratic republics, we still elect too many corrupt leaders, but at least we have the ability to share information and make leadership changes.

My immediate goal was to kick the Bush administration out of power. The wars in Afghanistan and Iraq were not going well. Photos of American troops torturing Iraqi prisoners made things worse. The Bush administration misled us into costly wars and then made numerous decisions that extended the losses. There was no doubt in my mind that electing a new president was the top priority.

The 2004 presidential election was between Republican President George W. Bush and Democratic U.S. Senator John Kerry. Senator Kerry served in the military during the Vietnam War. He introduced his 2004 presidential campaign by saying he was a military veteran reporting for duty.

The wars in Vietnam, Afghanistan, and Iraq were tragically similar. The wars began with patriotic calls to support the country as our troops defended America and the world. People felt proud to support war efforts to defeat evil monsters in distant lands. They ridiculed and attacked anyone who opposed the wars. Then the wars in Vietnam, Afghanistan, and Iraq ended up being very costly. The wars lasted much longer than expected. After many years of bad news, most people in the United States finally agreed the wars were costly mistakes.

John Kerry was famous for coming home after serving in Vietnam and saying, "How do you ask a man to be the last man to die for a mistake?" Conservatives called him a traitor as he tried to protect his military friends who were dying in large numbers in a war that was not going well.

John Kerry was correct about the war in Vietnam not going well. He was also correct during the 2004 presidential campaign to say the Bush administration was making huge mistakes in Iraq and Afghanistan. Was the country ready to accept the truth? Most conservatives were not. They ignored the huge costs of war and demanded patriotic support for President Bush and the war efforts.

Most Democrats opposed the war in Iraq. A majority of Democrats in the House of Representatives voted against authorization for the war in Iraq. In the Senate, President Bush lobbied for votes by saying he only wanted war authorization as a bargaining chip to use in negotiations with Iraq. He said the threat of war would help get more weapons inspectors into Iraq. Some Democratic senators voted for war authorization to be used for negotiations while saying in their speeches that invading Iraq was a bad idea. After the vote, we found out Bush lied to the senators as he quickly ended negotiations, told the weapons inspectors to leave, and invaded Iraq.

The 2004 presidential election pitted conservative war supporters against liberals who wanted the wars to end. Opposing an American war during a presidential campaign is not easy. John Kerry's status as a military veteran who served in Vietnam didn't protect him from vicious attacks.

Conservatives didn't want the election to be a referendum on the wars. The wars were not going well. Conservatives focused instead on destroying Senator Kerry. Conservatives used millions of dollars from a few wealthy donors to create a political front group called Swift Boat Veterans for Truth. They attacked Kerry by calling him an unpatriotic liar in thousands of advertisements. The attacks were so damaging that people still use the term "swiftboating" when talking about false claims designed to destroy a political candidate.

I wanted to kick the Bush administration out of power, but I wasn't sure what I could do to help. I was posting information about the wars in Iraq and Afghanistan on websites and in newspaper comment sections. I was called unpatriotic, and worse, over and over. Instead of talking about the wars, Bush supporters would attack me personally. I started to feel like I was being swiftboated with aggressive attacks, just like Kerry was.

We needed to stop these costly wars, but conservatives focused on launching vicious attacks instead of discussing the facts. I once again felt powerless. It seemed impossible to stop the wars. It seemed impossible to make a difference in elections dominated by wealthy front groups.

I ran for state assembly after a Republican candidate attacked future Senator Tammy Baldwin. Now I was seeing Republicans launch personal attacks with million-dollar ad campaigns funded by wealthy donors. What chance did I have to make a difference in politics compared to such well-funded political groups?

George W. Bush won the 2004 presidential election and continued to lose the wars. Wealthy oil company executives from Texas bought their way into political office and used the power of the U.S. military to steal oil on the other side of the planet. In addition to the costly wars, President Bush signed huge tax cuts into law that mostly helped the wealthy. When budget deficits started to rise from the wars and tax cuts, Republicans demanded the reduction of education and healthcare funding.

I considered myself a moderate Republican when I was younger, but after Republicans misled us into costly wars, I started supporting Democrats. I still wanted to stop wars, but to do that, I needed to stop warmongers from buying their way into office. To do that, we needed to pass campaign finance reforms. To get campaign finance reforms, we needed to elect more Democrats.

Wisconsin Senator Russ Feingold joined with Arizona Senator John McCain to pass bipartisan campaign finance reforms in 2002. Unfortunately, conservative Supreme Court justices later overturned some of the more important reforms in the *Citizens United v. Federal Election Commission* case.

While John McCain and a few other Republicans supported campaign finance reforms, most Republicans opposed them. Democrats have proposed many campaign finance reforms over the years. Republicans often block them while offering no proposals of their own. On the issue of campaign finance reform, Republicans are the problem.

When I ran for state assembly, I appreciated the matching funds the state of Wisconsin provided to candidates like myself. Still, I knew any future campaign would be lost before it began if I could not raise millions of dollars. Lots of great people decide not to run for political office because they are not personally wealthy. This makes our leadership less representative of the people.

When people donate to campaigns, there are contribution limits we must follow, but wealthy candidates are allowed to donate as much money as they want to their own campaigns. Wealthy "self-funder" candidates have a better chance to win elections with the millions of dollars they can donate to themselves. We should pass campaign finance reforms to apply campaign contribution limits to everyone, including the candidates.

If a wealthy person doesn't want to run for office, they often set up a front group to buy attack ads without anyone knowing who they are. Democrats have tried to pass reforms to increase the transparency of these anonymous billionaire front groups, but Republicans continue to block reforms.

If millions of dollars are needed to run for office, then only wealthy people will be elected as our leaders. Sometimes a leader won't be personally wealthy, but they will get the money needed to win elections by doing or saying anything that pleases wealthy donors. This makes the United States more of a plutocratic republic (ruled by the rich) than a democratic republic (ruled by the people).

The candidate with the most money doesn't always win, but they have incredible advantages over candidates with less money. Sometimes a candidate is so charismatic they can defeat a well-funded candidate, but even charismatic candidates need a lot of money to have a chance of winning in a money-drenched political system.

CHAPTER 9

PRESIDENT BARACK OBAMA

The wars in Iraq and Afghanistan weighed heavily on me. I grew up wanting to protect people from the brutalities of war, but now I found myself living in a time of war. I needed to know the details of the wars so I could convince people we should end them. I spent many years reading daily war reports. I saw the pain and suffering the wars caused. It took a toll on my mental health.

Before the wars started, my older brother left the military to go to school. He earned a master's degree and became a counselor at a Veterans Administration clinic in northern Wisconsin. He started meeting with former soldiers who experienced horrific events in Iraq and Afghanistan. I was worried about my brother suffering from stress disorders after listening to the stories and struggles of his patients.

The people most at risk of developing traumatic stress disorders are the troops and civilians in the war zones. Many veterans have unfortunately committed suicide. The pain and trauma of war overwhelm them. The same is true for kids and other civilians in war zones and refugees worldwide. One of the saddest parts of wars is seeing pictures drawn by young children expressing their fears of being bombed, killed, or forced to flee their homes. The trauma stays with them their entire lives. War is terrible.

Many people in the United States were stressed by the constant bad news coming from Iraq and Afghanistan. People all over the country were starting to oppose the wars. Conservatives still attacked anyone who spoke out against them, but even some conservatives admitted the wars were too costly.

The 2008 election was another battle between conservative supporters of the wars and liberals who wanted the troops to come home. The Republican candidate was Arizona Senator John McCain. I respected Senator McCain for his past military service, his partnership with Senator Russ Feingold to promote campaign finance reforms, and his respectful nature during political debates. However, John McCain was a warmonger I strongly opposed.

McCain wanted to send more troops to Iraq and Afghanistan. U.S. General David Petraeus had successfully tested a "surge" strategy in parts of Iraq. McCain wanted to expand the surge strategy throughout Iraq and Afghanistan. Most people agreed we would control more areas of Iraq and Afghanistan by sending more troops and money. The real question was, how long should we continue spending trillions of dollars to defeat, control, and bribe the local populations? We had already spent years trying to do it at a very high cost.

Americans started to agree the most patriotic thing to do was to support our troops by bringing them home. People finally rejected the false patriotism test from Republicans that said we must support wars if we want to be considered patriotic. After cheerleading three costly wars in Vietnam, Afghanistan, and Iraq, hopefully, Republicans will learn this lesson soon.

I was worried John McCain would win the 2008 presidential election and continue the wars. It was easy for a Republican candidate to wave the American flag and talk about the need for American strength and victories. It was difficult for Democratic candidates to explain how opposing wars was more patriotic and a better way to support the troops.

I'm not sure how the 2008 presidential election would have gone if it was only based on the wars. My guess is Republicans would have won again. However, in 2007, the economy started to crash. Most Americans were worried about the wars but were far more worried about their economic security.

Unstable investments in the housing market caused the economic crash that started in 2007. Wall Street banks were getting rich by selling thousands of home mortgages to investors. As long as people paid their monthly mortgage payments, the investment products would continue making profits for investors.

Wall Street banks wanted lots of home mortgages to bundle into investment packages to sell to investors. They started giving larger commissions to mortgage brokers to generate more mortgages. In many cases, these were predatory home loans, preying on home buyers excited about qualifying for a much bigger loan than expected. Wall Street banks also lowered the standards for who qualified to get mortgages. These were called subprime mortgages.

Republicans claimed the 2007 economic crash was caused by the government forcing Wall Street banks to lower their standards through an old 1977 law called the Community Reinvestment Act (CRA). However, many Wall Street banks that took on subprime loans were not part of the CRA program. The Wall Street banks also pushed risky loans in the commercial real estate market, which was not part of the CRA program. It wasn't an old law that crashed the economy. It was Wall Street banks making very risky bets.

When the economy started to crash, many people could no longer pay their mortgage payments. This not only hurt the people being kicked out of their homes, but it also hurt the Wall Street banks, which made huge bets on people being able to pay their monthly mortgage payments.

The economy was crashing. The wars were not going well. Americans were ready for a change in leadership. Democrats had a good chance of winning the 2008 presidential election. All we needed was a good candidate.

The obvious choice was Hillary Clinton. She was married to former President Bill Clinton and had been involved in politics for many years. She was very well known. I didn't like the idea of our presidents being from only two families for a couple of decades. Presidents Bush, Clinton, Bush, and Clinton seemed more like a royal monarchy with kings and queens than a democratic republic.

A presidential candidate who started gaining momentum was Illinois U.S. Senator Barack Hussein Obama. I really liked him, but I couldn't believe our potential presidential candidate had a name that sounded similar to Saddam Hussein in Iraq and Osama bin Laden from al-Qaeda. Republicans would have an easy time presenting their candidate as a flag-waving, patriotic Republican versus a "terrorist-loving" Democrat who wasn't even a real American. Of course, nothing was further from the truth.

Senator Obama gave a speech a few years earlier about how we are not a red America and a blue America but the United States of America. He was inspirational and focused on leading by the power of our example rather than through the power of our military. He talked about respecting, empowering, and including everyone in our communities. America was ready for the hope and change being offered by Senator Obama.

Republicans raised a lot of money to attack Senator Obama. They tried to destroy him personally and politically. Some progressive activists were upset when Senator Obama raised millions of dollars from wealthy individuals to defend himself. However, if Democrats only accept small donations as Republicans continue to benefit from millionaire candidates and billionaire-funded front groups, will Democrats ever have a chance to win elections and pass campaign finance reforms? It was a question I started asking myself.

Senator Obama probably would have lost the election if he hadn't raised enough money to compete with the well-funded conservative groups attacking him. The Obama campaign greatly expanded the amount of money raised from small donors through online platforms, but it still wasn't enough to compete with the wealthy donors funding Republican campaigns. Senator Obama's decision to accept large donations from wealthy donors made a difference in the election's outcome.

Republicans and Democrats both raised lots of money from wealthy Wall Street bankers. I was concerned this would lead to corruption. However, each party still had different approaches to Wall Street. Republicans helped Wall Street bankers get more freedom to take on bigger risks (and bigger scams) by reducing regulations. In fact, that was why the economy had just crashed in 2007. On the other hand, President Obama set up a consumer protection agency led by progressive reformer Elizabeth Warren to improve the fairness of loans, investments, and banking. That's a big difference.

Even if specific favors are not granted to big donors, big money in politics still corrupts democratic republics. Since politicians need to spend so much time talking to wealthy donors, they will primarily hear the concerns of wealthy donors. Politicians often won't respond personally to a parent worried about clean drinking water, but they will return the calls of wealthy industrialist donors who pollute the water.

I'm never thrilled about big money in politics, but I was thrilled to see Obama win the 2008 presidential election. It was the first time I felt it was worth having Democratic candidates raise money from wealthy individuals to win elections in the money-drenched system. We were proposing campaign finance reforms, but Republicans were blocking them. I didn't see any other way to achieve campaign finance reforms than to win elections and power within the current system.

I felt really bad for President Obama on his first day in office. President Bush handed him two costly wars while the economy was crashing. The national debt was spiking, and millions of people had just lost their jobs. It was one of the worst situations a new American president was ever handed. Since the economic collapse had been so devastating, some economists predicted another Great Depression like the one America endured in the 1930s. The country was a total mess when President Bush left office.

Of course, Republicans blamed everything on President Obama. The fiscal conservatives who had just cut taxes for the wealthy while misleading us into two costly wars were now suddenly concerned about the national debt. They started organizing "Tea Party" protests to blame President Obama for the huge increase in the national debt.

The debt spike was caused by costly wars and a massive loss of tax revenue when eight million people lost their jobs in the huge pre-Obama economic crash. People no longer had incomes and no longer paid income taxes. This massive reduction in tax revenue increased yearly deficits.

As conservatives blamed President Obama for the problems handed to him, the Obama administration went to work solving the problems. The Obama administration raised taxes on wealthy individuals, increasing the tax revenue. The nation was also adding millions of jobs, leading to more people paying income taxes. With more tax revenue being generated, the yearly deficits got smaller.

On the spending side, the Obama administration drastically reduced the costs of the wars. It wasn't an immediate withdrawal, but many steps were taken to reduce our military involvement and spending. Military expenses and deaths were lowered significantly by the time President Obama left office.

As the economy improved and the costs of war were reduced, the yearly deficits continued to get smaller. The Tea Party protests ended, and most conservative news outlets started to ignore the national debt issue they used to scream about on a nightly basis.

While Republicans were intensely opposed to President Obama, Democrats were mostly tired of politics after spending years opposing the Bush administration. After a political party wins a big election, its supporters tend to feel they can finally take a break. On the other hand, the voters who lost the election are upset and determined to organize themselves politically to win the next election. This is why we often see political momentum swing back and forth.

Republicans were fired up and ready to vote Democrats out of office in the 2010 midterm elections. Independents were leaning toward voting for Republicans as they struggled financially due to the huge economic crash. It's frustrating when people blame current politicians for the economic problems caused by former politicians and then vote the same politicians who caused the issues back into office.

Republicans also had long-term voting trends that helped them win the 2010 midterm elections. Many Republicans are older people who tend to vote in all elections. Democrats have older voters too, but we also have lots of student and low-income voters who don't vote as often. They tend to vote in the presidential elections every four years but often stay home during midterm elections.

I was one of the Democrats who was exhausted after opposing the Bush administration for eight years. The wars were still going on, and the economy had just fallen off a cliff, but I had confidence in the decisions being made by President Obama. I no longer felt like I needed to be engaged in politics as much. It felt good to take a break.

CHAPTER 10

DEATH THREATS

I was fortunate to be economically secure through the huge 2008 economic crash. We had moved from Colorado back to Madison, Wisconsin, a few years earlier to start our family. My wife worked for a small, rapidly growing healthcare software company. When our two children were born in 2008 and 2009, we decided I would stay home and take care of the kids instead of paying for childcare.

Being a stay-at-home dad was not something I ever expected to do in my life, but it was a great experience. Instead of reading books about politics and websites, I started reading books about childhood development and food allergies. Taking care of young children is a full-time job with many challenges, but it also includes incredible experiences.

It was the perfect time to be with my kids. I was relieved the Bush administration was no longer in power. I felt like the country and world were heading in a better direction. I still spent time defending President Obama online, but my main focus was raising my kids.

On a nice summer day, I went for a walk with my one-year-old son strapped to my back. We often went for walks like this, but on this day, we came across a long path full of political protesters chanting slogans. They were walking to a rally at the state capitol in Madison.

It was one of the first Tea Party protests in my area, with conservatives upset about the national debt spiking. I was walking along the side of the protesters when I asked them in a loud voice where they had been for the past few years. I asked the protesters why they were silent as Bush cut taxes for the wealthy and misled us into two costly wars. A few of the protesters agreed, but most of them just yelled partisan attacks at me. I decided I should walk away since some of them seemed pretty riled up, and I had my one-year-old son sitting in a carrier on my back. I figured it was safer to stick to online political debates.

I found it easy to defend President Obama online because the facts showed the economy improving and the yearly budget deficits getting smaller. I had the same interaction with many conservatives on a daily basis. They would blame President Obama for "destroying America," and then I would respond with facts showing how President Obama was handed many problems that were now being fixed. Then the conservatives would ignore the facts and attack me personally.

While I knew how to respond to conservatives who didn't know the facts, I had no idea how to respond to conservatives who were only interested in launching rude, racist, and ridiculous attacks on President Obama. There was a segment of conservatives who seemed to have gone off the deep end with their hatred for President Obama.

When I was opposing the costly wars, I was often called unpatriotic by conservatives, but none of them ever threatened to kill me. Now I was being attacked with death threats by a small segment of conservatives.

Some of the conservatives on the message boards insisted President Obama was a Muslim who was determined to destroy America. Conservative media outlets pushed conspiracy theories to keep Republicans engaged and enraged.

For my safety, I changed my name on message boards and social media sites to something anonymous. I used random pictures instead of using a picture of myself. I was protecting myself and removing conservatives' ability to respond with personal attacks as I was trying to focus on facts.

One area I was not anonymous was on my websites. My name and address were on the website domain name registration records. A Republican was losing many debates on one of my political websites. The Republican started to launch vicious attacks. I banned the person from the website, but they must have found my name on the website domain name registration records because they started posting death threats on one of my business websites.

Conservatives were starting to post more radical conspiracy theories and threats, but this person focused their anger directly on me. The person knew my address, had looked through my Facebook posts, and knew everything about my family. The person said I needed to shut down my "anti-American" political website or else my children would be killed.

At this point, both of my children were toddlers. I was taking care of them as a stay-at-home dad while I worked on my business and political websites. My kids were everything to me, so this threat sent me into a panic. I knew the chance of the threat being real was very low. This person was just using threats to try to get me to stop supporting President Obama.

I wasn't sure if I should tell my wife someone was threatening to kill our kids. I didn't want to alarm her, especially since I thought there was only a tiny chance the threat was real. However, conservative posts had become more radicalized and violent after President Obama was elected, so I wanted my wife to be aware and alert when she was with the kids in the neighborhood.

The next time the conservative posted on one of my websites, he said he was in a car near the baseball field two blocks from my house. In most cases, this would have been a horrifying threat causing me to call the police while locking my kids in the house. However, it was actually good news because the baseball field had been replaced by a city swimming pool. The person must have been looking at an outdated map or picture when he made the threat. It was a relief to find out the attacker was not in my neighborhood.

I reported the incident to the local police department, but there wasn't much they could do. We didn't know who the person was. The police didn't sound like they would start an in-depth investigation. Since the person was posting the threats on one of my websites, I could track the person's IP address, which gave me some basic information about his location. I replied to one of his threatening posts with a message about how I contacted the police, and we had the IP address from his location just north of New York City. This must have scared the person away because I never heard from him again.

Getting death threats is a life-changing experience. It's like going for a pleasant walk down a nice path and then being told a mentally unstable person with a gun might be waiting for you somewhere along the path. Your pleasant walk is never the same. I took more precautions, but there was no way conservatives were going to scare me out of politics.

I continued to proudly defend President Obama and the progress that was being made. While the facts showed progress, the country was still recovering from the massive 2008 economic crash. Since most of the effects of the pre-Obama economic crash were not felt until President Obama took office, many people blamed President Obama. The 2010 midterm elections were a disaster for Democrats, with Republicans winning control of Congress and many elections for governor in numerous states.

I had been focused on wars, foreign policy, and national politics for the past few years, but suddenly Wisconsin had a new Republican governor named Scott Walker. He was caught on tape telling one of his billionaire donors he would keep wages low with a "divide and conquer" strategy to trick working people into supporting wage cuts. He caught my attention when he started attacking teachers like my mom.

CHAPTER 11

GOVERNOR SCOTT WALKER

Wisconsin Governor Scott Walker pretended to support working people but he was lying. Scott Walker claimed to be "one of us" by posting pictures of his bag lunches and Harley Davidson motorcycle, but it was just political propaganda. His political career was based on pleasing billionaire donors by keeping wages low.

Billionaire donors often oppose workers' rights. They don't like forty-hour workweeks, safety standards, and breaks during a ten-hour shift. These things all reduce the amount of money they make. That's why they support corrupt politicians like Scott Walker, who are willing to attack workers' rights in exchange for campaign cash.

Governor Scott Walker started attacking public sector workers such as teachers, social workers, and highway snow plow drivers. His goal was to reduce public sector compensation and workers' rights (which would also put downward pressure on private sector wages and rights). Scott Walker's "divide and conquer" strategy was based on making private sector employees jealous of public sector employees.

Scott Walker started saying public sector employees have very good benefits that are better than what private sector employees have. Governor Walker didn't tell people that public sector employees may have better benefits but they also have lower wages. When you combine the benefits and wages, the total compensation packages were fairly average compared to those of private sector workers in similar jobs. Prior governors were often hesitant to increase wages (that would impact the current budget), so they gave public sector employees raises in the form of better benefits (that impact future budgets).

If Walker had been honest, he would have admitted public sector and private sector employees have similar total compensation packages when compared to similar jobs. Since Scott Walker was a corrupt politician trying to help his billionaire donors keep wages low, he misled people into thinking teachers and other public sector employees were making too much money. In addition to lowering compensation packages, the governor was also trying to end the collective bargaining rights of public sector employees.

Needless to say, many of us in Wisconsin were not happy our teachers and other public sector workers were being unfairly attacked by the billionaire puppet Scott Walker and his fellow Republicans. We were featured in the national news as over 100,000 of us showed up at the capitol in Madison to let Republicans know we support our teachers and other public sector employees.

I was taking care of my young children at the time, but I still found ways to support the public sector workers. I would drive around Capitol Square with my kids sitting in their car seats drinking their afternoon yogurt cups. I would honk the horn to the beat of, "This is what democracy looks like!" Then the crowd of thousands would repeat the chant. The kids would roar with laughter and say, "Do it again, Daddy. Do it again!"

On the day 100,000 people marched in Madison, I joined the crowd on Capitol Square after I was done taking care of the kids. It was snowing and cold, yet warm and inviting since everyone was so welcoming and supportive of each other. There were a lot of teachers in the crowd, but also private sector union members and firefighter unions. It was great to see one of my firefighter friends at the capitol with his family.

Governor Walker said he wouldn't apply the compensation cuts to firefighters and police officers. Most of these employees are men who tend to vote for Republicans. However, the governor had no problem cutting the pay of mostly women teachers who tend to vote for Democrats. It was great to see my firefighter friend and his fellow firefighter union members leading the marches in support of public sector employees (with bagpipes!).

For the next few evenings, I spent time inside the capitol supporting public sector workers. The entire capitol was full of people singing and chanting from the central rotunda to the staircases and balconies on every floor. The police said it was one of the most peaceful protests they had ever witnessed.

Since I had daddy day care duties to attend to each morning, I never spent an entire night in the capitol like many people did. I suppose they all should have been charged with trespassing, but nobody attacked the Capitol Police or damaged anything (other than some tape marks on the walls from signs). We were there to show our support for workers peacefully as the Republican governor was attacking workers' rights.

My focus was shifting from national politics to state politics. I supported Democrats in national elections because Republicans were misleading soldiers like my dad and brother into corrupt and brutal wars. Now I was supporting Democrats on the state level to stop Republicans from attacking teachers like my mom.

Since I was usually home with my kids, I relied on Twitter to get updates from the capitol. I followed the accounts of journalists, politicians, union leaders, and supporters at the capitol. I had been posting online for years, but this was the first time I saw the power and potential of online political organizing.

Twitter allowed me to keep track of what was happening at the state capitol while also participating. The #wiunion hashtag made it easy to find and connect with people. I wanted to be at the capitol the entire time, but as a stay-at-home dad, my only option was to support public sector employees through social media posts when the kids took their afternoon naps.

Our efforts were not successful. I was reminded that politicians have the power to do dreadful things once they are elected to office. Scott Walker was able to cut the compensation packages of public sector workers while stripping them of their bargaining rights. Democratic state assembly members delayed the vote by traveling to Illinois (votes can only be held when enough state assembly members are present in Madison), but the delay didn't lead any Republicans to support public sector workers. The Republicans cheered as they voted to take compensation and rights away from teachers, social workers, snow plow drivers, etc.

A lot of people in Wisconsin came to the same realization I had. It was difficult to stop politicians from making bad decisions once they won elections. The focus needed to be on keeping corrupt politicians out of office. Scott Walker motivated thousands of Democrats to get involved in Wisconsin politics. We didn't want billionaire puppets like Scott Walker making dishonest decisions that hurt our families, friends, and neighbors.

People wanted Scott Walker out of office as quickly as possible. They found out they could recall the governor if they got enough signatures to initiate a recall election. All across Wisconsin, we started seeing people standing on street corners collecting signatures to recall Governor Scott Walker. Many working people were not happy with Scott Walker's attacks on their rights. Enough signatures were collected within a few weeks to schedule a recall election.

The recall election was a threat to Scott Walker's power, but it also led to a lot of campaign contributions for him. Wisconsin state law allows a governor facing a recall election to raise unlimited amounts of money. The challenger, however, still has to follow the $10,000 individual donation limit. The 1987 law basically encourages corrupt campaign fundraising by the governor and needs to be changed.

An investigation from *The Guardian* newspaper showed emails from Scott Walker's campaign staff saying the governor should get on a private jet and visit billionaires all over the country to ask for million-dollar donations. Since the Wisconsin recall election was the only major election happening anywhere in the United States during the summer of 2012, Scott Walker had no problem raising money from billionaires all over the country.

Sometimes these billionaires would donate directly to Scott Walker's campaign, meaning their names would appear in campaign finance reports. If they wanted to hide, then Scott Walker would tell the billionaires which anonymous political front group they should donate to. Of course, his favorite front group was the one his former campaign staffers had recently set up.

The United States Supreme Court said there was little chance of corruption by allowing political front groups to raise unlimited amounts of money. The justices said there would be a "wall of separation" between the candidates and the front groups. Does Scott Walker telling billionaire donors to give money to the front group run by his former campaign staffers sound like a "wall of separation"?

In addition to the money flowing into Scott Walker's campaign and front group, his wealthy supporters set up anonymous front groups to flood Wisconsin airwaves with campaign ads. The ads didn't even try to defend Scott Walker. The billionaire donors pummeled Wisconsin for weeks with ads about how recall elections are not the "Wisconsin way." The ads were well funded and very effective.

Scott Walker won the recall election. Thousands of Wisconsin Democrats tried to make a difference in the spring and summer of 2012, but we were defeated by a corrupt politician being propped up by billionaire donors from all over the country. Lots of us felt powerless. Scott Walker continued to attack workers' rights and mislead Wisconsin voters while remaining a favorite of billionaire donors.

Scott Walker was making me restless. I wanted to do something to make a difference. I wanted to stop Republicans who were misleading us into wars on the national level and attacking workers' rights on the state level.

Social media gave me an outlet for being politically active while taking care of my kids. It allowed me to reach thousands of people very easily and cheaply. I figured my best chance to make a difference was posting on social media during the kids' naps and when they were watching a movie. I had no idea if my time on social media would make a difference, but my options were limited.

CHAPTER 12

#YOUJUSTPULLEDAROMNEY

After receiving a few online death threats, I decided to create an anonymous Twitter account for posting about politics. I decided "Peace is Active" would be the account's name. I wanted to disrupt the narrative of peace activists being viewed as weak pacifists. I want peace activists to be seen as active, strong, smart, diplomatic people doing their best to stop wars before and after they begin so we all can live in peace. I want peace activists to be active, not passive.

Conservative accounts on Twitter made fun of me for only having ten followers, but my account soon grew to ten thousand followers as I connected with great people all over the world. As my account was getting bigger, it was easier to get my posts to trend on national hashtags. I was also trying to create my own hashtags to see if I could get them to trend on the national list.

During the 2012 presidential election, President Barack Obama was running for reelection. He spent his first term in office dealing with the terrible economic crash and the wars he inherited. Wealthy Republican Mitt Romney was the Republican candidate running against President

Obama. The polls showed a close race.

I wasn't sure if there was anything a stay-at-home dad could do to influence the presidential election. I was trying to make a difference by posting on social media. My goal was to have one of my hashtags appear on the national trends list. Posting on social media seemed like my best chance to make a difference as I waited for the mac and cheese water to boil.

When I was growing up, I enjoyed watching comedy shows. A memorable routine from Jeff Foxworthy went, "You might be a redneck if ..." and then he would joke about homes that move and cars that don't. I didn't like the term "redneck," but I found out "redneck" was first used as a reference to workers in the mines of West Virginia. They wore red handkerchiefs around their neck to let everyone know they supported the miners union. Instead of making fun of workers, I used a similar format to make jokes about wealthy Republican presidential candidate Mitt Romney.

I started posting with the hashtag #YouJustPulledARomney. A few of my social media followers began posting their own jokes on the hashtag. After a few hours, lots of people were posting on the hashtag with variations of the format. "If you think Wall Street is more important than Main Street ... #YouJustPulledARomney." Another one I remember was, "If your only foreign policy experience is visiting Swiss banks ... #YouJustPulledARomney." The hashtag was catching on and started to trend nationally. I was excited and kept posting anything I could think of to increase the number of posts per minute.

When #YouJustPulledARomney started trending nationally, huge celebrity accounts began posting their own jokes with the hashtag. I got a big kick from comedian Will Ferrell posting a joke on the tag.

Thousands saw his post. It was incredible to think that something I had started a few hours earlier led to one of my favorite comedians posting a joke on the hashtag. Someone named Ethan Cox posted, "If Twitter is good for anything, it is snidely pointing out that the emperor has no clothes. Check out neat hashtag: #YouJustPulledARomney."

The hashtag went all the way to the number one spot on the national trending list and stayed there for most of Saturday night, September 15, 2012. Lots of celebrities and large political accounts posted on the hashtag. It was just a few weeks before the 2012 presidential election. I watched it happen with a feeling of pride and disbelief.

The next day, I was thrilled to read tons of great posts that were posted on the hashtag while I was sleeping. I checked the latest posts and noticed a lot of people were still using the hashtag. I started posting again to see if I could get it trending nationally again. It rose all the way to number one on the national trending list for a second night in a row on Sunday, September 16. I wasn't sure if a stay-at-home dad could make a difference, but here I was, a few weeks before the presidential election, influencing the national conversation from my couch.

The next day, a news magazine called *Mother Jones* released a video of Mitt Romney saying half the country votes for Democrats because they are dependent on the government. The quote played into the image of Romney as a wealthy Republican who looked down on people who needed assistance, many of whom were his Republican supporters.

When Romney said half of Americans depend on the government, he included full-time workers who are paid so little they still qualify for assistance. Instead of attacking full-time workers who need assistance, Republicans should increase the minimum wage so corporations feed full-time workers instead of making taxpayers do it.

If you tell your supporters they're losers, #YouJustPulledARomney.

Many people used the hashtag when sharing the Mitt Romney video on social media. The hashtag started trending again but didn't reach the top of the national trending list for the third time. However, over a four-day period, over eighteen thousand posts were generated, and over seventeen million people saw them. That type of media exposure is something billionaire front groups pay huge amounts of money for, but I did it organically, for free.

I found a way to make a difference, but there was no guarantee I would be successful. Most of my hashtags never caught on. Millions of people seeing jokes about Mitt Romney a few weeks before the election was a major success in my mind. However, it was still a very small event compared to the millions of dollars wealthy donors spent on campaign ads.

I still thought it was worth my time and effort. I live in a state where most elections are won by a few thousand votes. Some people ask if they can really make a difference if they talk to a hundred people and only convince one extra person to vote. Is that worth it? Well, in a swing state like Wisconsin, if there are ten thousand volunteers across the state who each convince one person to vote, then those ten thousand votes could swing the entire national presidential election.

I don't know if my online efforts impacted the election, but I felt I made a difference in my own unique way. I was excited when President Obama was reelected for another four-year term. He continued to reduce our involvement in the wars while building a stronger economy at home. He was a respectful and successful president I was proud to support.

After the 2012 election, my focus turned back to state politics. Defeating Governor Scott Walker was my primary focus. Since I was taking care of my kids every day, social media was still my best option for involvement. I was determined to help elect a new Wisconsin governor in the 2014 election.

CHAPTER 13

@NEWWISGOV

Some people wondered if anyone would run against Wisconsin Governor Scott Walker. He was likely to win, so why would anyone put themselves through the stress of a political campaign just to lose? People said the same thing when former Governor Tommy Thompson was running for office. I heard a story about a Wisconsin Democrat named Ed Garvey who knew he would probably lose but ran for governor against Tommy Thompson in 1998 to stand up for Democratic principles.

I started thinking about doing the same thing. I hoped someone else would run against Scott Walker, but nobody was making any announcements. No Democratic candidate was countering Scott Walker's daily dose of nonsense. I created a Twitter account with the goal of electing a new Wisconsin governor. I called it @NewWisGov and started connecting with other political accounts in Wisconsin.

I sent out a post saying I was thinking about running for governor, but I wanted to explore the decision while posting from an anonymous Twitter account. People started following @NewWisGov as I posted daily about why Scott Walker needed to be kicked out of office in the 2014 election. I sometimes responded directly to Scott Walker's posts to point out how the governor was misleading people.

A few months later, Mary Burke announced she was running for governor to defeat Scott Walker. She was part of the family that started the Trek Bicycle Corporation. She had worked at the family business to expand its operations in Europe. She was also involved with many charitable organizations in Wisconsin. I liked her and was very happy I would not need to run for governor.

During the 2014 campaign, @NewWisGov grew to have thousands of followers. My posts were often featured on Wisconsin hashtags during important political events. I noticed my posts with political cartoons did the best, so I continued to communicate visually along with written messages. We organized direct message rooms on Twitter where online activists would coordinate and share messages to amplify.

My kids were getting older, and it was getting easier to post on social media during the day. Watching my kids smile and play reminded me why I was trying to defeat the governor who attacked Wisconsin teachers. Watching my kids grow reminded me why we needed to keep the water clean and provide access to healthcare. Watching my kids go to school for the first time reminded me why we must keep our communities and schools safe.

A few months before the 2014 governor election, I went to the state convention for the Democratic Party of Wisconsin. It was the first time I had gone to a political convention. Seeing and meeting politically active people from all over the state was awesome. I enjoyed saying hello to Senator Tammy Baldwin as she poured me a Spotted Cow beer from a keg during her meet-and-greet party.

During one of the main sessions of the convention, I saw the communications director for the Democratic Party of Wisconsin standing in the back of the convention hall. I didn't know her, but I followed her social media accounts. I asked her if there were any specific topics she wanted social media activists to push. She looked at me and said, "Are you @NewWisGov?" That's when I knew my social media posts were making a difference. She said she wanted me to keep up the good work, and gave me some ideas and resources.

Mary Burke was rising in the polls. I started to think we could defeat Scott Walker and his billionaire donors. It was still an uphill battle, but there was hope. Democratic activists like me were the underdogs in the fight. Scott Walker was a messaging machine. Republicans had majorities in both chambers of the legislative branch after using gerrymandering software to give themselves a majority of the seats with a minority of votes. Republicans had the power to direct the political conversation in Wisconsin. They were also getting better at using social media for messaging purposes.

Wisconsin Republicans used the hashtag #UWslushfund to cut funding for the University of Wisconsin. You might already be asking why the University of Wisconsin has a slush fund. That is the power of messaging! Lots of people in Wisconsin were asking that question as Republican politicians and activists all started using the #UWslushfund hashtag on the same day. It started trending on the state trends list in Wisconsin.

The University of Wisconsin has a savings fund designed to save money for large projects such as new buildings. All major universities have a similar savings fund. Instead of praising the university for good fiscal management and planning, Republicans used the savings fund to claim UW had a large slush fund and didn't need more funding. Before journalists had time to tell everyone the savings fund was good fiscal policy and average in size compared to other universities, Republicans had already voted to cut the funding for the University of Wisconsin.

Another trick Republicans used was the promotion of a tuition freeze. Politicians who truly support students and universities would fund the university so tuition levels could remain reasonable. However, as Republicans cut education funding, universities are forced to raise tuition. Governor Scott Walker used a tuition freeze as another way to restrict funding for the University of Wisconsin while bragging to students he was doing them a favor.

Scott Walker had no interest in being honest. He had no interest in talking about issues such as workers' rights or education funding. His main goal in the 2014 campaign for governor was to destroy Democratic governor candidate Mary Burke. The problem was that she was a really nice and sincere person. It was very difficult for Scott Walker and his billionaire donors to turn sweet Mary Burke into a monster. Then the "scandal" happened.

When Mary Burke was putting her campaign together, her staff created a document that outlined all of the policy positions she would support as governor. One of her campaign staffers inserted a few paragraphs into the campaign document explaining why we should raise the minimum wage. The campaign staffer had originally written the paragraphs a few years earlier for a different candidate.

Political campaigns should be about how we can move our communities forward, not about how a campaign staffer writes a campaign document. There are some great political journalists in Wisconsin, but a few focus on "gotcha" moments instead of real issues. After reading "news" reports about a campaign staffer using the same paragraphs for two different political campaigns, Scott Walker's campaign created ads that attacked Mary Burke for this "outrageous" act of plagiarism. Instead of having a political debate about the future of Wisconsin, Scott Walker and his wealthy donors focused the entire campaign on this phony plagiarism issue.

Scott Walker won the election. I was not a happy camper. I was getting sick of phony scandals being the focus of our politics instead of real issues. Wealthy donors were dominating our political system. They were using their money to distract and divide voters at the national and state levels.

I enjoyed being involved with politics through my social media accounts, but my impact on campaigns was nowhere near the impact multi-million dollar ad campaigns could have. My kids were growing up fast and would start going to school soon. I was thinking about getting back into the workforce. I still had no idea what my "real" job would be. I wanted to stay involved with politics. I wanted to keep making a difference in my own unique ways. I enjoyed being with my kids, but I was ready to get more involved.

CHAPTER 14

DEMOCRATIC PARTY OF WISCONSIN

The first time both kids were in school, I didn't know what to do with myself. It was so quiet in the house. After years of full-time parenting, it was liberating to have a few hours each day with no immediate child care duties.

I wasn't able to get a full-time job since I still had parenting duties before and after the kids' half-day pre-k and kindergarten classes. My dream of being hired by the 2016 Russ Feingold senate campaign wasn't an option. I continued to post on social media when the kids were at school, but I knew I could start doing more.

I attended the monthly meetings and events organized by the Democratic Party in my county. At one meeting, there was an update from the Democratic Party of Wisconsin executive director. He said they were looking for people to volunteer at the state party headquarters near the capitol.

After the meeting, I waited to speak with the executive director and told him I could volunteer five days a week. The office was a fifteen-minute bike ride from my house with a bus route available during the winter. I started volunteering at the headquarters of the Democratic Party of Wisconsin.

Everyone at the state party was great. I found my tribe. Everyone who worked there was trying to make a difference in their own unique ways.

Most people working in politics have a specific reason that drives them to work long hours in stressful campaigns. For me, it was growing up in a military family. For someone else, it was a loved one dying after being cheated by insurance companies. For another, it was a deep commitment to clean drinking water. Many employees had personal reasons to work for Democrats as they fought for civil rights, immigrant rights, women's rights, LGBTQ+ rights, workers' rights, etc. We all had our reasons for being there. We all had our reasons for entering the crazy life of politics and campaigns.

The Democratic Party of Wisconsin was on the second floor of an old building. The conference room had a great view of Madison's Capitol Square from the floor-to-ceiling windows. Near the second-floor entrance was a large open area where volunteers and interns worked. About ten offices surrounded the open area. When I started, there was one person in each office, but as we got closer to the election, there were often three or four people in each office.

I was processing donations that were mailed to us. I would open the envelopes, make copies of each check, and then enter the donor's information into a database. More importantly, I was meeting people and discussing ways we could win elections. I heard stories about people all over the state creating neighborhood volunteer teams during the campaigns for President Obama. The state party was trying to support these neighborhood volunteer teams. It was easier to keep them active year round rather than rebuilding them each election cycle.

Supporting neighborhood volunteer teams was important, but it was very expensive. Every donation I processed allowed the state party to support more teams. It made me feel like I was an important part of the operation, even though I was only volunteering a few hours each day.

The state party also raised money online with a new payment processing company called ActBlue. The great thing about ActBlue was once a donor entered their credit card information, they could easily donate to any Democratic campaign in the country. It was like a food delivery app that makes spending money at many different restaurants easy. People are less likely to donate to a campaign if they have to type in their credit card number each time. ActBlue greatly increased donations from small donors to Democratic campaigns and state parties.

ActBlue also allowed state parties and campaigns to raise more small-dollar donations without needing to hire more people. If a Republican campaign gets a million-dollar check from one of their billionaire donors, it takes one employee to record the information and deposit the check at the bank. If a Democratic campaign raises a million dollars from thousands of small donations, it takes an army of employees and volunteers to open the envelopes, record the information, make photocopies of the checks, etc. With ActBlue, thousands of donations could be processed by one employee uploading a spreadsheet with a few minutes of work.

I really enjoyed volunteering at the Democratic Party of Wisconsin. I decided I would try to get a job there. I could start part-time and then go full-time when the kids were both in school all day. I wanted to work on a campaign, but working at the state party seemed more stable in terms of supporting my family.

Politics is a risky career choice for parents. Campaigns always end with most people laid off after the election. The loss of income and healthcare is tough for young staffers but even worse for parents who have kids on a family healthcare plan purchased through a campaign that no longer exists.

The Democratic Party of Wisconsin (DPW) was a year-round organization, but it still hired a lot of people during election years and laid off almost everyone after each election. Getting a job there was not a stable career choice, but I wanted to get more involved with politics. I already had a foot in the door as a volunteer.

When a part-time financial assistant quit his job, I was asked if I could volunteer more hours each week. I told them I was looking for a paid part-time job while the kids were in school. They posted the job, and I went through the interview process. They hired me as a part-time financial assistant in the operations department.

I loved my new job. After dropping the kids off at school, I would race to the state party headquarters to do as much work as possible before racing back to pick up the kids. The Broadway musical *Hamilton* includes a song about being "in the room where it happened." That's how I felt when I went to staff meetings. I was in the room where campaign strategy and issues were being discussed. I loved every minute of it. Sometimes my manager would remind me that a part-time financial assistant doesn't have to be involved in every discussion, but I had years worth of ideas I wanted to share.

One of the first ideas I pushed at the state party (as a part-time financial assistant) was to change the name of the state party. Decades of tradition and thousands of dollars worth of rebranding made this an uphill battle. However, I had spent the previous few years supporting the state party on social media. I knew we had a branding problem.

Each summer, the hashtag for the state convention was always something like #DPW2016 with the updated year. Many people wondered if the hashtag was about the Department of Public Works. I wanted to call the state party "WisDems" with the convention hashtag #WisDems17. Our website was already wisdems.org, and our Twitter account was already @WisDems. It was time to retire DPW as our branding.

When I brought up the name change idea in a staff meeting, the party's leadership laughed about people thinking we were the Department of Public Works. They had heard that before too. However, it was decided most people had known us as DPW for many decades, and it would be very costly to change our branding. We had more important work to focus on.

CHAPTER 15

2016 PRESIDENTIAL ELECTION

Most of our meetings at the Democratic Party of Wisconsin focused on electing a Democratic president in 2016. We weren't sure if Vice President Joe Biden would run for president or maybe it would be Secretary of State Hillary Clinton. We were trying to support as many neighborhood volunteer teams as possible. Wisconsin elections are always close, so we needed lots of volunteers to help mobilize our voters.

Republicans generated a long list of "scandals" to attack Democrats. They attacked Hillary Clinton after the deaths of four Americans in Benghazi, Libya. The Republican attacks on Hillary Clinton were inaccurate, but that didn't stop them from relentlessly pushing their nonsense. Republicans politicized the Benghazi deaths in an attempt to stop Hillary Clinton from running for president in 2016.

Before the Benghazi attack, a video posted on YouTube ridiculed Muslims. There were protests in multiple cities, with the largest protest happening in Cairo, Egypt. Libya was in the midst of a civil war with many heavily armed militias spread throughout the country. While protests were happening worldwide, a Libyan militia attacked the American consulate in Benghazi, Libya, killing the American ambassador and three other people.

There was no advanced warning of the Benghazi attack. It was over before military reinforcements could be sent. Some of the Americans escaped and went to a nearby CIA station. Many hours later, satellite images showed Libyan militias advancing toward the CIA station. Many Americans were successfully evacuated to the airport.

Benghazi was a tragic event, but there was no reason to blame President Obama and Secretary of State Hillary Clinton. Republicans concluded two years of congressional hearings by admitting all proper military procedures were followed during and after the Benghazi tragedy. Republicans politicized the deaths of Americans to attack President Obama and the potential next Democratic president, Hillary Clinton.

I was really mad about Republicans politicizing Benghazi for political purposes. I wondered why they never held hearings about the costly wars in Iraq and Afghanistan. If they were so concerned about the "Benghazi 4," then why weren't Republicans holding hearings about more than four thousand American troops killed in Iraq?

Republicans created another scandal by demanding to see President Obama's birth certificate. It was a nonsense issue Republicans used to make President Obama seem foreign. They said he was an illegitimate president because American presidents must be born in the United States of America. President Obama showed a copy of his birth certificate to prove he was born in Hawaii. Republicans asking the first Black president to show his papers was deplorable.

One of the biggest "birthers" pushing the birth certificate conspiracy theory was New York City real estate developer Donald J. Trump. He was on a television show called *The Apprentice*. Since I was still interested in starting my own business, I enjoyed watching *The Apprentice* to see how contestants would handle the weekly sales and marketing challenges. If the contestants did a bad job, Donald Trump would decide which contestant to fire with his catchphrase, "You're fired!"

When Donald Trump started attacking President Obama, I stopped watching *The Apprentice*. I had no intention of supporting Republicans who were attacking President Obama. I enjoyed watching President Obama get revenge at an annual dinner for journalists where he told jokes about Donald Trump while he was sitting in the audience. As enjoyable as it was to watch, that was probably one of the moments that convinced Donald Trump he would run for president.

Donald Trump announced his campaign for president with a hateful tone. He attacked a lot of people, but he focused on immigrants and refugees who were trying to reach America in search of a better life for their families. Trump said they were mostly rapists and murderers. It reminded me of attacks on Irish immigrants with last names like mine a few generations earlier.

Trump's ability to whip up fear and rage toward other people reminded me of the Bush administration scaring Americans into supporting the war in Iraq. I quickly realized Donald Trump was willing to say or do anything to get elected. Nobody took him seriously as a candidate, but he knew how to rile up the Republican base with attacks, over-the-top bragging, and fear-mongering.

During the Republican presidential primary, Donald Trump used the televised debates to roast the other Republican candidates. He put on a ratings-boosting show where he attacked the other candidates in ways most of us had never seen before. He was brutal in his attacks and unprofessional in his delivery. We never knew what he was going to say next.

Trump was an outsider who had never run for office before. He organized a populist campaign that attacked the Republican establishment and the overall political system. He said it was time for a disrupter like him to shake things up and make some changes. He said it was time for everyone to stop being so politically correct. People were drawn to his message and campaign.

Donald Trump was running as a Republican but sounded like a Democrat. I was confused when Trump said he would "drain the swamp" in Washington, D.C., since Republicans opposed campaign finance reforms. Donald Trump had never advocated for policies that would help normal Americans. He was known for suing everyone and not paying contractors he hired. His corrupt track record of being "charitable" was mainly a history of using charity money to help himself.

Donald Trump was having an impact on the national discussion. People were drawn to his populist message. Unfortunately, while the hatred Trump generated was real, the promises Trump made were fake.

There are two types of populist campaigns. The first type of populism is national populism. National populists say our loved ones will only be safe by defeating all other types of people. The goal is to rally supporters by whipping up fear and rage directed at other people. This is why Trump used racist language to attack immigrants and

Muslims. Trump's populist campaign was based on fear, racism, white nationalism, and the pumped-up image of an alpha male who would be the ultimate protector. Vladimir Putin used the same type of national populism in Russia.

The other type of populism is progressive populism. Progressive populists support the pursuit of happiness with the goal of liberty and justice for all. Democrats often promote this type of populism with proposals for increased education funding, better wages, and affordable access to healthcare. Rather than the authoritarian dictatorships of national populism, progressive populism promotes transparent and accountable forms of government. Instead of vilifying other people, progressive populism sees diversity as a natural and strong foundation of our existence.

Senator Bernie Sanders from Vermont ran for president in the 2016 Democratic presidential primary to promote progressive populism. He railed against the Washington, D.C., establishment like Trump did, but without the racist, national populism Trump was pushing. Economically, many Americans felt insecure. Millions of people were crushed by the huge economic crash. Automation of factories and political corruption continued to increase the gap between rich and poor. Railing against elites worked for both Bernie Sanders on the left and Donald Trump on the right. However, Democrats were the only ones supporting campaign finance reforms and raising the minimum wage. Trump was lying.

As the presidential primary elections went on, it was unbelievable that Donald Trump was winning the Republican race. Most Republicans tried to play nice with Trump, only to be destroyed by him later in the primary. Some Republican candidates tried directly confronting Donald Trump, but nobody survived a confrontation with the political bully.

Huge crowds were starting to show up at Trump campaign rallies. Most wore red campaign hats with the slogan, "Make America Great Again."

On the Democratic side, Hillary Clinton won most of the Southern states during the Super Tuesday primary election. Most political nerds knew at that point Hillary Clinton would be the nominee. Democrats award delegates based on the percentage of votes won. That makes it difficult to catch up to someone once they have a significant lead. On the Republican side, they use a winner-take-all system where all state delegates are awarded to the winner even if a candidate only wins by one percent. This makes it easier for a candidate in the Republican primary to catch up by winning a big state like California or Texas toward the end of the primary. For Democrats, we were at the point where there wasn't much of a chance that Bernie Sanders would catch up to Hillary Clinton.

As the primary battle was ending, I was using my social media accounts to promote unity. We needed to come together to defeat Donald Trump. Polls showed that most people who supported Bernie Sanders planned to vote for Hillary Clinton. Still, some large social media accounts were talking about supporting Trump, the Green Party, or not voting as a form of protest.

I tried to debate these large social media accounts by telling them Democrats were the only ones supporting campaign finance reforms and workers' rights. Voting for the Green Party (as I did with Nader in 2000, from Colorado, which wasn't a swing state at the time, but still, never again) or protesting the two-party system by not voting only helps Republicans. In the 2016 campaign, progressives and Green Party members who didn't vote for Hillary Clinton helped Republicans set back progressive goals for decades. Trump appointed three Supreme Court justices who all oppose campaign finance reforms. The lifetime

Supreme Court appointments often span three decades. It was a major loss for progressive populists.

I understand the desire to vote for the best candidate (see my vote for Ralph Nader above). However, I now realize it makes no sense to feel good about myself being pure and principled if my vote for a third-party candidate helps Republicans win elections. If we want to make progress, we need to win elections in our current two-party system. That is the reality we are dealing with.

The more elections we win, the more progress we can achieve. We win elections in liberal areas very easily. Those victories are not enough. We need to win elections in every part of the country, especially in moderate swing states during presidential elections. Policies that are very popular in liberal areas might not bc as popular in swing states. We need activists to keep pushing us forward, but we also need to ensure we win elections in moderate swing states.

There was enthusiasm for Hillary Clinton in large liberal cities in 2016, but when I traveled to rural areas or lower-income areas, there was momentum for Donald Trump. People needed someone to fight for them. Trump promised to do it with fake promises that sounded great.

I didn't think Trump could win. I hoped he wouldn't win. I knew he was a con man. I was working part-time at the state party to help Democrats win elections. In the evenings, I would post on social media to encourage everyone to vote for Democrats.

I was still annoyed by some large social media accounts attacking Hillary Clinton or supporting Donald Trump. I made lists of these large accounts on Twitter to track people I wanted to debate with. I had a list of conservative Twitter accounts that allowed me to peek into a completely different reality where everyone was on the Trump train. I also made a list of far-left accounts supporting the Green Party or encouraging people to protest the two-party system by not voting.

I didn't know that some of the large social media accounts I was debating were Russian intelligence agents.

The investigation into Russian meddling in the 2016 presidential election included the names of social media accounts I debated. One account was pretending to be a Black activist opposed to Hillary Clinton. Another Russian account was a conservative account with over 100,000 followers. I thought it was the official Tennessee Republican Party account, but it was just a large account with the name @TEN_GOP. The social media accounts operated by Russian intelligence agents generated lots of retweets and messaging wins to help Donald Trump.

Russian agents were also purchasing advertisements on Facebook to influence people. Lots of Americans saw these ads and social media posts. The Russian disinformation operation was very successful.

I debated a lot of people over the years, but I never thought I would interact with Russian agents meddling in our elections. Their goal was to elect Trump because they thought he was chaotic and compromised in many ways. They wanted to fan the flames of division in America to weaken us. Social media posts and Facebook ads weren't the only way Russia tried to meddle in the 2016 presidential election. The Russians ended up playing a key role in helping Trump win.

CHAPTER 16

BREAKING NEWS

"Donald Trump Grabs Women Without Permission"

Donald Trump was accused of sexual assault by many women over the years. He always denied it. Now there was a video of him bragging about sexually assaulting women. Most people thought this was the end of Donald Trump's presidential campaign.

A few hours after the recording was released, a bunch of leaked emails from Hillary Clinton's campaign hit the news. That was very convenient timing for Donald Trump!

We later found out Russian agents had stolen the emails. The stolen emails were sent to a website called WikiLeaks. One of Trump's advisors, Roger Stone, knew about the emails and demanded that Wikileaks release them immediately after Trump's sexual assault recording was released. The goal was to distract everyone from Donald Trump admitting he sexually assaulted women.

About a half hour after Roger Stone demanded the emails be released, WikiLeaks released the emails. The release of this Russian propaganda into the American election news cycle was very effective. It distracted people from Donald Trump admitting he gropes women without permission.

It was odd that Roger Stone knew about the emails Russia had stolen. It was odd that Trump's campaign manager, Paul Manafort, had worked with Ukraine's former Russian puppet leader. It was odd that Trump stood next to Russian dictator Vladimir Putin in Helsinki and told the world there was no reason to think Putin meddled in the election even though American intelligence agencies had just confirmed that Putin had meddled in the election. We're still not sure how connected the Trump campaign was with Russian efforts, but the Russians saved his hide when their propaganda was released shortly after Trump was caught bragging about sexually assaulting women.

American media companies split time between the Trump sexual assault recording and the emails leaked from Hillary Clinton's campaign. Over the next few weeks, the media started to focus on the email story as more emails stolen by Russian agents were released. The story about a presidential candidate admitting he sexually assaulted women faded away.

After the Russians were done releasing the stolen emails, the Trump campaign started to focus attention on an FBI inquiry into the email practices of Hillary Clinton. The investigation found no wrongdoing by Hillary Clinton. She kept classified emails on the classified servers while keeping her personal emails on her system at her house. A few classified emails were found on her personal system, but they were not marked correctly, so there was no way for her to know.

Even though no wrongdoing was found, FBI Director James Comey announced shortly before the election that a few more emails were found on a different computer. He announced he was reopening the Hillary Clinton investigation. This dominated news coverage and encouraged Donald Trump to lead his followers in chants of "Lock her up" at his campaign rallies right up until election day. Once again, no wrongdoing was found by the FBI. Still, the media mostly ignored the announcement of innocence a few days before the election compared to how intense the coverage was when the FBI reopened the investigation.

Russian meddling, Republican FBI Director James Comey, and the media all played a role in making Donald Trump the president of the United States.

CHAPTER 17

STOMACH ACHE

I spent election day in 2016 reminding people to vote for Hillary Clinton and U.S. Senate candidate Russ Feingold. Madison is a very liberal city, so any effort to remind people to vote in Madison can generate lots of extra votes for Democrats. I was posting on social media with one hand and waving Democratic campaign signs with the other hand while standing on a busy street corner for many hours.

After the polls closed, I was still confident Hillary Clinton would be the next president and Russ Feingold would win the Senate election. The Senate election was a rematch of the 2010 election that Republican U.S. Senator Ron Johnson won as part of the Republican Tea Party wave. Senator Johnson had shown himself to be a conspiracy-minded buffoon. Johnson married into a very wealthy family and spent a ton of money on campaign ads, but I still didn't think he could defeat Russ Feingold again.

I started getting nervous about the numbers as I refreshed the newsfeed on my phone. Hillary Clinton had more votes, but the election was still very close in the swing states. I then saw a prediction that Trump would win the Electoral College while losing the overall popular vote.

It was the first time the nightmare of Trump being president of the United States entered my mind.

I felt sick. It felt like someone punched me in the gut. Trump was going to be our president? This couldn't be real. I was embarrassed for our nation. I was sad. I was in a state of shock.

Senator Johnson defeated Russ Feingold. I couldn't believe it. It was one of the worst election nights I ever experienced. Trump won Wisconsin by a very small margin of 22,748 votes out of close to three million votes cast. Hillary Clinton got more votes nationwide, but Donald Trump won enough swing states to win the Electoral College. The con man sexual assaulter was moving into the White House.

The next day, I went to my job at the Democratic Party of Wisconsin. We had a staff meeting where people were in shock. Some people were crying. Trump promised to kick millions of people off healthcare. He promised to appoint very right-wing Supreme Court justices. Some of us knew people in the DACA program for immigrant children who were brought to this country when they were very young. The fear was President Trump would round up the children and send them to countries they don't remember. There was a lot of sadness and worry in the room.

After taking office, President Trump turned his hateful campaign rhetoric into cruel policies. He separated children from their parents at the border. He said the cruel action would convince other people not to come to America. I was embarrassed to have a president using such abhorrent policies. Republicans said President Obama took custody of children too, but the Obama policy was to separate and protect children if they were not with family members. President Trump changed the policy to separate all children, even if they were with their parents.

Centuries ago, we didn't tell boatloads of European immigrants to turn around and go home. The United States of America welcomed European immigrants and documented them. The immigrants contributed to the strength of our nation in many ways. The Statue of Liberty says, "Give me your tired, your poor, your huddled masses yearning to be free." We've always been a nation of immigrants.

By upgrading official border crossings with Mexico, we can welcome immigrants where they should be welcomed and documented. This means fewer people will try to cross illegally through other areas of the border. Improving official border crossings allows the border patrol to focus on drug and gun smugglers trying to cross illegally instead of dealing with asylum seekers who were told the official border crossings were closed.

American farms need seasonal workers. Many of the workers cross the border. Document these people and stop demonizing them. Stop demonizing family members and asylum seekers. Immigrants have a lower crime rate than native-born Americans. Some of the largest companies in America were started by immigrants. Unfortunately, that didn't stop President Trump from describing immigrants as rapists and murderers.

Hatred toward immigrants is not the answer to any of our problems. National populists like Donald Trump use economic despair to generate hatred toward immigrants. Conservatives want us to be mad at other people. They don't want us to be mad at the free market economic system or the corporate executives who fund their campaigns.

Should we be mad at Chinese workers for "taking" our jobs? A corporate executive once said he prefers Chinese labor because they want to work, while Americans are lazy. Do they really want to work long hours, or are they being forced into harsh working conditions by a dictatorship restricting workers' rights? Chinese workers recently started a workers' rights movement that overwhelmed the Chinese censors for a brief time. The movement was called "996.ICU" with a chant that roughly translated to, "Working 9 a.m. to 9 p.m. six days per week will send you to the intensive care unit." Many people in China were forced to work seventy-two hours per week.

Working conditions in the United States used to include long working hours and sweatshop labor conditions, but we used the protections of our democratic republic to organize fellow workers and push for workers' rights. American labor unions achieved a "955" working system where most people work forty hours per week, five days per week. Sometimes people work longer hours, but laws require extra pay if extra hours are worked.

Instead of blaming workers in other countries for taking our jobs, let's support their efforts to achieve more democracy and workers' rights. Corporate executives continue to prove they will move jobs to locations that allow abusive forms of labor. Politicians often channel our economic frustrations into hatred toward other workers. We need to stop falling for this divide and conquer strategy.

A large number of job losses recently have been caused by the automation of factories. People are being replaced by robots. The people who came to Wisconsin to work in the factories along the shores of Lake Michigan no longer have good-paying factory jobs like they used to. The same is true in most industrial areas. Instead of blaming immigrants, robots, or local mayors for the economic despair many people are in, we should join progressive populists in demanding an economy that achieves liberty and justice for all. We shouldn't punish humans for losing jobs to robots. Robots doing work for us should be a good thing.

If you're worried about jobs going to other countries, support workers' rights worldwide. Corporations try to make bigger profits by finding the cheapest forms of labor. Shaming and boycotting corporations into no longer using abusive forms of labor in other countries can be effective, but some corporations have no shame. We need to support workers' rights in all countries.

Unfortunately, supporting workers' rights all over the world won't solve the problem of corporations using automation and robotics to replace our jobs. That's why we need to support human rights around the globe. We're getting to the point where a few wealthy individuals will own the robotic production of our economy, along with drone armies able to conquer any area of the planet. These wealthy robot and drone owners should not rule over us or force us into poverty. Technology can free us rather than force us into poverty.

We shouldn't restrict access to doctors and medicine just because a family member lost a job. Communities shouldn't spiral into despair and drug abuse whenever corporate executives decide the jobs in our communities are no longer needed. Job losses are often not our fault. Don't punish me by taking away access to my child's asthma medication. He still needs to breathe while I find a new job.

This doesn't mean we don't have a responsibility to support ourselves, but we shouldn't lose access to healthcare if we lose our job or decide to leave a job. Conservatives say this cruelty is designed to make sure we get another job right away, but it takes time to find a new job. Why should people lose access to doctors because they are between jobs? Healthcare should not be tied to our jobs. If we want a vibrant and flexible economy, we need to update policies designed generations ago when our grandparents stayed at the same job their entire lives.

Are we communists or socialists if we want to smooth out the cruelties of the market system? No. Most of us like market-based economic systems that allow us to start businesses and buy the products we want. We also like using our democratic republics to consider values other than market values.

For example, most of us think all children should have access to education, not just kids with parents who can afford it. That doesn't mean we are communists who hate the free market. It means we realize market systems are successful for some things but incapable of educating kids living in impoverished areas. We can choose to use our democratic republics to make sure all kids have access to education. Social Security, Medicare, unemployment insurance, the Affordable Care Act, and many other American programs have eased some of the economic cruelties of the market system.

Huge corporate farms are now pushing out generations of Wisconsin farmers. Robots are pushing out generations of Wisconsin factory workers. Blaming immigrants won't help. Blaming robots won't help. Turning to drugs and alcohol won't help. The only thing that helps is supporting a fair and peaceful system for everyone.

Some argue our team must win by conquering all other teams, but that just leads to wars and misery. We have the ability to compete peacefully in fair market systems. We can use our democratic republics to provide a safety net during times of economic distress. We have the ability to be safe and secure in sustainable ways. We have the ability to live in peace.

Unfortunately, the election of Donald Trump made some people feel justified in blaming others. Instead of realizing we're all on the same team, some people continued to attack other people. White nationalists were very happy Trump was elected. Many of them posted messages saying one of their own was now in power.

After Trump took office, white nationalists marched with torches in Charlottesville, Virginia, at a "Unite the Right" rally, shouting, "You will not replace us!" Some of them could be heard chanting, "Jews will not replace us!" The white nationalists got into fights with people who were protesting their march. The conflict led to a woman being killed when a white nationalist rammed his car into a crowd of people.

When asked about the violence, President Trump said there were "very fine people" on both sides. People marching with a group chanting, "Jews will not replace us!" are not very fine people.

Law enforcement agencies said white nationalists were committing most acts of terrorism in the country. Militia groups were growing larger and connecting with each other. Not every Republican was a white nationalist, but most white nationalists supported Trump.

All of this made me sick to my stomach. The election of Donald Trump meant more attacks on immigrants, more white nationalist groups, more conservative Supreme Court justices who oppose campaign finance reforms, and possibly the loss of access to doctors and medicine for millions of Americans. My country was represented by a serial liar who admitted he sexually assaults women. I was embarrassed and sad for America.

The 2016 election was over. Lots of people at the state party were laid off. We tried keeping as many field organizers as possible to keep in touch with neighborhood volunteer teams, but we returned to being a very small staff at the state party. Since we still needed to raise money and process a lot of donations, I got to keep my job. I was depressed about the 2016 election outcome but was more determined than ever to ensure we never lost another election in swing state Wisconsin.

CHAPTER 18

SOUTH MADISON VOTERS

I wanted to work full-time at the Democratic Party of Wisconsin, but the kids needed to be picked up from school shortly after three in the afternoon, making it hard to have a full-time job. I really wanted to spend my time working to defeat Governor Scott Walker and President Donald Trump. I felt this was what I had been preparing for my entire life. I was in the right place at the right time to make a difference.

My wife and I talked about switching roles roughly halfway through the kids' childhood, with her staying home as the primary caretaker and me getting a full-time job. She wanted to spend more time with our kids. I wanted to dive headfirst into a political career. We decided to make the switch.

My salary at the state party was nowhere near the software company salary we had enjoyed for many years. I had jobs before, but this was the first time I had a job while being responsible for housing and feeding my family. I had a wave of panic come over me when I thought about possibly getting laid off after the next election.

I was promoted from being a part-time financial assistant to a full-time office manager at the Democratic Party of Wisconsin. I still processed donations, but I also made sure everything in the office was working. I became an expert in printers, copiers, carpet cleaners, and the dreaded dungeon storage rooms in the creepy basement. My role on the financial operations team expanded to include bank deposits, monthly Federal Election Commission reports, ActBlue uploads, new employee onboarding, and many other tasks.

I sat at the front desk and welcomed people as they came into the office. Most of the visitors were elected leaders who used our office to make fundraising phone calls. I met everyone who visited the office. I felt like I was in the center of the political world.

Since I had received death threats from right-wing political activists in the past, I started to think about security procedures at the office. If a gunman came into our office, I would be the first person in the line of fire sitting at the front desk. We had key fobs to enter the office after hours, but the property management company kept the door unlocked during the day. I noticed there was no way for me to lock the door even if I needed to.

A few months later, a man broke into a gun shop and stole a lot of weapons. He released a manifesto declaring his intention to kill as many politicians as possible. He was an hour south of Madison in Janesville when he stole the weapons. The Capitol Square in Madison was the nearest collection of politicians to his location. Our office location was easy to find online. People in the office were scared. My position at the front desk took on new meaning as the police spent ten days searching for the heavily armed man.

During those ten days, I thought about buying a bulletproof vest and a handgun. If sitting at the front desk made me the security guard, then

I wanted to be prepared. We had a plan for what employees would do in case of an attack, but I thought firing a few shots at the attacker might slow him down to give the employees more time to get to safety. We had a sign on the front door saying no guns were allowed, but I was pretty sure the attacker would ignore the sign while shooting me.

I grew up hunting and shooting guns with my dad and brothers. Like most Democrats, I support gun ownership as long as we have background checks to limit who can purchase guns. Hunters in northern Wisconsin are not the problem. People buying guns for self-protection are not the problem. People buying guns for sport shooting are not the problem. The problem is domestic abusers, criminals, and mentally unstable people having access to guns. Background checks won't stop all gun violence, but they help save lives.

We can also save lives by limiting the type of weapons purchased. All countries have mental health issues, domestic abuse, and people living in poverty, but mass shootings mostly happen in the United States. The main difference in the United States is we allow the purchase of military-style weapons by the general public. Sometimes a background check isn't even required if the weapons are purchased from another person rather than from a store.

Americans love guns. We buy a lot of them. Having so many guns in our homes makes it more likely our anger, depression, or intoxication could lead to gun violence. Too many children die after shooting themselves or siblings when an unsecured gun is found in the home. While murders and mass shootings get most of the news coverage, suicides make up a large number of gun deaths each year. We must find ways for people to feel happy, respected, powerful, and secure without needing so many guns.

We know we can reduce gun violence by reducing poverty. As awful as mass shootings are, they represent a small percentage of gun deaths in the United States. Gun violence mostly happens in areas where crime and drugs are rampant due to a lack of jobs. Over half of yearly gun-related deaths are in high-poverty areas. Young men use guns to feel powerful in a world that makes them feel powerless. Farmers and factory workers are losing jobs in rural, urban, and suburban areas. Poverty leads to all sorts of problems, including gun violence.

We can end poverty at any time. We don't have to force people to live in poverty when they lose jobs or have a personal crisis. Many law enforcement officers support anti-poverty programs to fix the crime and violence they face in high-poverty areas. Some sheriffs ask why taxpayers pay so much to police high-poverty areas when anti-poverty programs are cheaper and have been shown to be more effective. This is where the "Defund the Police" movement originally came from. It wasn't a total defunding of police, but the idea was to spend more taxpayer money on anti-poverty programs instead of spending so much on police and jails.

The man who stole the weapons and threatened politicians was caught in a remote area of Wisconsin. I never bought a bulletproof vest or brought a gun to the office. We were relieved there was no longer a threat of that person showing up at our office. Other scary people would sometimes show up at the Democratic Party of Wisconsin office, but they were mostly harmless. Some of the visitors were homeless people with cognitive issues. Some visitors were people with very strong opinions they wanted to share. I would listen to their concerns while walking them down the steps and out the front door. I got so good at it that the official procedure for dealing with unusual visitors was "Go get Tom."

Answering the phone at the Democratic Party of Wisconsin was also an interesting experience. I'm not sure why Republicans call the Democratic Party so much, but they do. I decided to track the front desk calls in a spreadsheet. Republicans were just over half the calls. Since I had been debating conservatives online for many years, I enjoyed the chance to speak directly with them. Some of them would engage in respectful debate, but most of them would just yell obscenities. We decided to use an automated phone system to help avoid the Republican calls.

My favorite people to see at the front desk were the field organizers. They were a great group of passionate people who worked very hard while having a good time doing it. One of the organizers was in charge of creating a neighborhood volunteer team in my neighborhood. Like a good field organizer, he recruited me to get involved.

My neighborhood on the south side of Madison had a volunteer team during the Obama campaigns, but the team was no longer active. I contacted the former leader of the group. She told me her friends were getting too old to volunteer. I wanted to see what a volunteer neighborhood team looked like, but I didn't realize the field organizer needed me to help build a team from scratch. I wanted to hide in my house and never take calls from the field organizer ever again, but then I remembered we saw each other in the state party office at least once a week. There was no turning back. I was going to help the field organizer build a neighborhood volunteer team.

We had lists of Democratic supporters in the South Madison area with phone numbers and addresses. We started calling the supporters to invite them to a meeting for new volunteers. After calling hundreds of people, four people showed up at the first meeting. We decided to call ourselves the South Madison Voters. Over eighty percent of the people in the South Madison neighborhoods are Democrats. We just needed to make sure they voted. The new volunteers helped us call more people to invite them to the next meeting.

I was used to calling strangers since I had a phone sales job after college. The field organizer had a lot of great tips for how to recruit volunteers. For example, when asking people to volunteer, they would often say no. However, by asking if they wanted to volunteer at 9 a.m. or 3 p.m. on Saturday, they would usually pick one of the times and sometimes show up.

I was working full-time at the state party and had young children to help care for in the evenings. I was posting on social media as much as I could. I didn't have time to lead a neighborhood volunteer team. Nobody did. We all pitched in as much as we could. I helped organize once-a-month door-knocking events. South Madison Voters continued to be a very small group of volunteers.

I knocked on a lot of doors when I ran for state assembly, so I was comfortable talking with strangers about politics. We had lists and maps of neighborhoods that directed us to homes where new people had recently moved in. Our goal was to have a short conversation with a few scripted questions to determine whether they were Democrats, Republicans, or independents. If they were Democrats, we made sure they knew when and where to vote. If they were independents, we continued to visit and speak with them. If they were Republicans, we would tell them to have a nice day.

I had a great experience my first time knocking on doors for South Madison Voters. A guy took out his phone and asked me to remind him when the next election was as he put it into his calendar. It reminded me of someone at the state party saying we can swing entire elections if we have ten thousand volunteers who all remind one extra person to vote. I already reminded someone to vote! I intended to knock on lots of doors to remind or convince more people to vote. It was something active I could do to make the world a better place. I was highly motivated to kick Governor Scott Walker and President Donald Trump out of office.

The neighborhoods in the South Madison area are diverse, with a lot of apartments. The area gets a lot of new residents from all over the country. In addition to making sure people knew where to vote, we also found ourselves telling people stories about how Governor Walker attacked teachers. We also told them how Governor Walker was wasting taxpayer money by offering four billion dollars to a foreign corporation called Foxconn, which was known for misleading people about future jobs in exchange for tax money. We were happy to discover most of the new residents were Democrats and opposed what Scott Walker was doing. We knew if we reminded lots of people in the South Madison area to vote, it might be the difference that could swing the entire election.

The importance of the South Madison area was confirmed when our neighborhood volunteer team was given a campaign office for the last few months before the 2018 election. Getting a campaign office was great, but it would also be a lot of work. Who would open and close the office each day? Who would sit there during the day? Our volunteer team was still fairly small. We all pitched in to keep the office open and operating, but for many of us, it was way more time than we had volunteered for, causing lots of stress.

I worked hard at the state party headquarters during the day while volunteering at the South Madison Voters campaign office in the evenings and on weekends. I was missing time with the kids, so I asked if they wanted to volunteer with me. They both enjoyed being at the campaign office. They helped take care of other kids during volunteer meetings. They enjoyed eating the food that had been donated. When I went out to knock on doors in the neighborhood, my daughter would sometimes ride her scooter with me. She enjoyed scooting ahead to look for the next house on my canvassing list. "Here it is, Daddy!" she would beam and then ask for the next address on the list.

I was knocking on a lot of doors, but it was obvious we needed more volunteers. We continued to hold volunteer events at the campaign office that sometimes included musicians and political leaders. People would show up for events, but not many people made calls or knocked on doors. We were preparing for a big rush of people to volunteer during the last four days before the election, but I was skeptical if volunteers would suddenly show up after not showing up for most of the year.

It was the Saturday morning before the 2018 election. A few volunteers were at the South Madison Voters' office getting ready for the final push to mobilize our voters. We had been calling lots of people, asking them to sign up for volunteer shifts during the final four days of the campaign. We were setting up training areas with walk packets for people who volunteered to knock on doors. We had a back room with tables set up for phone bank volunteers. Suddenly, we noticed it started to snow outside with strong wind gusts. The snow was blowing sideways rather than falling straight down. It was wet, heavy snow that made it miserable to be outside.

There was no way volunteers would show up to knock on doors during this wintry mess. All of our work to prepare the South Madison Voters' campaign office was probably a wasted effort. We were pretty upset.

I started to get depressed about another four years with Governor Scott Walker. Senator Tammy Baldwin was running for reelection, but she had a large lead in the polls. I was mostly concerned about the election for governor.

Then, volunteers we had never met before started coming into the office. Not just a few people, but more people than we expected! They wore snow boots, rain jackets, winter hats, and gloves. I should have known Wisconsin volunteers would not be deterred by snow and wind. We trained them, gave them maps, and sent them out into the neighborhoods as quickly as possible. Then we trained the next wave of volunteers. It was incredible to see so many volunteers come through the South Madison Voters' campaign office door that snowy November day.

The volunteers restored my faith in democracy. Volunteers for South Madison Voters worked hard for many months with no promise that our efforts would make a difference. Now we had lots of volunteers knocking on doors throughout our neighborhoods to remind Democrats to vote. The volunteers came back cold and tired, but they were happy to find people who needed a reminder to vote. We knew our efforts might determine the outcome if the election was close.

We were told our campaign office would host the final campaign stop for Democratic governor candidate Tony Evers and Senator Tammy Baldwin. It was a great event with lots of people stuffed into our campaign office. It was a great way to thank our volunteers. We knew the election was expected to be close, but the energy in our campaign office made us hopeful for victory.

On election day, we knocked on as many doors as possible to remind Democrats to vote. When our volunteer shifts ended, there was still an hour before the polls closed. I was determined to remind a few more people to vote. I took a roll of Senator Baldwin stickers to a grocery store and stood outside, offering stickers to people. If people didn't want a sticker, I told them to have a nice night. If they took a sticker, I figured they were Democrats, so I asked if they had voted yet. I found two more people who hadn't voted and were happy to hear their polling place was only a few blocks away.

Senator Tammy Baldwin won her election by a wide margin. The election for governor was another story. Defeating Governor Scott Walker would not be easy, but I felt we all did everything we could. There was an election night party at a theater on State Street in Madison. Before going to the campaign watch party, I decided to watch election results at a bar near the theater with a small group of friends.

Tony Evers was ahead in the governor election, but Scott Walker was getting closer with each update. I was getting nervous. I remembered the sick feeling I had after the 2016 election. Democrats all over the country did a lot of work, but it was all for nothing as Donald Trump won the presidency. That's how it works in politics. We do tons of work, and then we either win or lose, with the result often lasting four years. I hoped my volunteer efforts with South Madison Voters would help kick Scott Walker out of office.

People in the bar groaned when an election update showed Scott Walker had taken the lead. A random person sitting next to me didn't know I worked at the state party. He started complaining about how the Democratic Party is stupid and doesn't know how to win elections. I had to walk out of the bar. I needed to get away from that person and away from the election results. I walked down State Street, mumbling curse words to myself. So much work for nothing.

A few minutes later, a text message from a friend reminded me that the absentee ballots from Milwaukee County hadn't been released yet. Lots of Democrats live in Milwaukee County. There is a law in Wisconsin that says absentee ballot results can't be released until all absentee ballots in the county are counted. Since Milwaukee is a large county, they usually finish counting their absentee ballots late into the night. This isn't a conspiracy theory or a "mysterious late-night ballot dump" but rather the way Wisconsin law says these ballots should be counted and reported.

About an hour later, democratic candidate Tony Evers was declared the winner of the election for governor. It was a very close election, with Evers winning by one percent with a margin of 29,227 votes out of 2.6 million votes cast. We were exhausted, but we were very happy we won. It was quite a change from our feelings after the 2016 election. Many tears were shed again, but they were tears of joy this time.

We had a great time in the theater celebrating with campaign workers and volunteers. We had all spent the last few months of our lives doing everything we could to make a difference. Many of us had attended the protests after Scott Walker attacked teachers in 2011. We were so happy to finally see him get kicked out of office. Governor-elect Tony Evers and the new Lieutenant Governor-elect Mandela Barnes took the stage to thank all of us. It was a great celebration.

The sign on the outside of the theater was changed to say "Governor Tony Evers." Many of us were taking pictures in front of the sign when a field organizer hugged me and said, "Everything we all did made a difference!" I think about that a lot. The election was so close. It really did come down to everything we all did. Volunteers on neighborhood teams all over the state were determined to make a difference, and we did. Instead of having a governor who attacks teachers, we elected Governor Tony Evers, who used to be a teacher.

CHAPTER 19

WISDEMS FINANCE DIRECTOR

I was proud of the work I did with the South Madison Voters, but I needed to stop volunteering so much. I was taking on more responsibilities at the state party. Work projects sometimes kept me busy late into the night. During the 2018 campaign, I was asked to manage some fundraising programs at the state party. Shortly after the 2018 election, I was promoted to be the finance director in charge of all fundraising for the state party.

Many people at the state party were laid off after the 2018 election. I was happy to still have a job. My family would continue to have healthcare. My increased salary as finance director would give us more breathing room in our home budget. I was happy to be able to support my family, but I wondered what I had gotten myself into by accepting the role of finance director. I was already exhausted from everything I did during the 2018 campaign, but now I was taking on a huge challenge for the 2020 campaign.

During presidential elections, Wisconsin is one of the main swing states in the Electoral College. When I spoke to campaign workers in other states, they would often say, "Hey, Wisconsin, the future of the planet is riding on your shoulders!" Yikes! I laughed to myself about growing up wanting to make a difference. Now I was being told the future of the planet was riding on my shoulders. The pressure I felt was intense since I knew they were correct. The 2020 presidential election might come down to whether or not I could raise enough money to hire enough field organizers to defeat President Trump in swing state Wisconsin. I was determined to be successful in my new role.

I was reminded of Wisconsin's importance as a swing state when the Democratic Party awarded the 2020 national convention to Milwaukee. I was excited to go to my first national political convention, but I was hoping to go to Miami or North Carolina rather than just going an hour east to Milwaukee. Oh well, I was still excited to go to my first national political convention at the new Milwaukee Bucks arena. My excitement dimmed when I realized how much extra work would be involved as the finance director for the host state.

The role of finance director changed shortly before I accepted the role. Wisconsin Republicans removed donation limits from state parties in Wisconsin. They also made it legal for state parties to give unlimited amounts of money to candidates all over the state. These changes made state parties a primary hub for fundraising efforts. It also created a huge loophole for wealthy donors to get involved in Wisconsin politics. The amount of political money flowing into Wisconsin was about to explode.

Unlimited donations are an open door for billionaires to buy elections. There should always be donation limits so the mega-wealthy can't overwhelm our democratic system with massive amounts of money. I wanted campaign finance reforms, but Republicans were welcoming wealthy donors to Wisconsin. Since we had not achieved campaign finance reforms yet, my job was to compete with Republicans in the money-drenched system.

We had a list of wealthy donors who supported the Democratic Party of Wisconsin. We were calling them, but I noticed our wealthy donors were in the one thousand to ten thousand dollar donation range, while some Republican donors gave six-figure donations. This is why Republicans changed the laws to allow unlimited donations.

My plan was to raise record amounts of money from lots of small donors. I saw enormous potential in digital fundraising. The state party was just getting started with online donations, and there was much more to be done. My background with online businesses led me to begin testing social media fundraising and some paid advertising on Google.

I wasn't sure if we should keep the old direct mail fundraising program. Society was changing from paper checks to digital transactions. The state party needed to make changes too. Financially, the direct mail program was breaking even. Before killing off the direct mail program, I decided to send a letter to a list of addresses I created from our database of donors. My first letter was very profitable, so I continued sending letters. I tested a lot of ideas and continued to increase the profits. I set direct mail revenue records three years in a row. I got excited whenever a huge stack of donation envelopes arrived in the mail. As I was doing my happy direct mail dance, I would get the evil eye from one of my favorite financial operations employees who opened all the envelopes to process the checks. It reminded me to focus on digital fundraising.

I bought ads on Google to generate traffic to our ActBlue donation pages. I would test different headlines and donation requests to see what worked. Once I found a combination that worked, it would usually continue working as long as I could get more people to the donation page.

Most people reached our ActBlue donation pages through our email fundraising program. With Donald Trump as the president, we would just tell our email subscribers what crazy thing Trump did or said that day. Then we would remind them Wisconsin is one of the main swing states that will determine if Trump remains president for a second term. It was an easy sales pitch because it was true.

I've seen a lot of fundraising emails over the years, but it was different being the person sending them. I was confident I could create a good-looking email fundraising program with better graphics, pictures, videos, and stories. I tested a lot of different formats, but the winning format was always the same bare-bones email you get from all campaigns. We all use the same format because it works. The primary goal of the email fundraising list is to raise money to hire more field organizers.

I noticed with the email program that name recognition makes a difference. I asked Wisconsin Governor Tony Evers and a few other elected leaders to send emails to our list with the donations being split between the campaigns. We also sent emails from celebrities. One of the celebrities was Bradley Whitford from the television show *The West Wing*, who played the character Josh. I was a big fan of the show, so I was thrilled to find out he grew up in Madison and wanted to help the Democratic Party of Wisconsin.

As we got closer to November 2019, we planned a fundraising event called 1 Year 2 Win. We used the hashtag #1year2win on social media and recruited celebrities to post about how the presidential election would probably be decided in Wisconsin. Bradley Whitford, Debra Messing, Piper Perabo, and many other celebrity accounts posted messages and donation links. Some of the biggest fundraising bumps came from former Obama administration officials and elected leaders who had large lists of political followers. Their followers were more likely to have ActBlue accounts.

The most amazing part of the #1year2win fundraising campaign was a video made by Julia Louis-Dreyfus. She starred in shows such as *Seinfeld* and *VEEP*. It was a short video where she talked about how important Wisconsin would be in the presidential election. She allowed us to use it in Facebook ads to promote our fundraising links. We hired a consultant to run the Facebook ads. We were all amazed by how fast the donations came in from that video. It opened our eyes to the incredible potential and scale of digital fundraising.

The #1year2win campaign raised more money than we expected. My favorite financial operations employee showed me the thick ActBlue report and said, "Can you imagine if all of these donations were checks mailed to us? We'd be buried by envelopes!" We were entering a new phase of digital fundraising at the state party, and I was thrilled to be a part of it.

As we got closer to the election, it was impossible for me to do everything that needed to be done. We hired more people, including a new finance director to run the wealthy donor program. I was able to focus more on digital fundraising. I became the digital fundraising director.

After trying for a couple of years, my battle to change the organization's name was finally moving forward. We had a new employee in the communications department who really liked the idea. He made a great new WisDems logo for the state party. People really liked the new logo. Everyone was finally convinced it was time to change our branding. We replaced the old DPW logo with the new WisDems logo whenever we ordered materials from the printer we used. I was a happy camper when I slapped a WisDems bumper sticker on my car.

CHAPTER 20

PANDEMIC VOTING

As the calendar turned to 2020, we heard about a virus causing sickness and death in China. President Donald Trump told us there were only fifteen cases of the virus in the United States, and the number would soon go down to zero. Cases started to increase in California and New York as infected people from China and Europe arrived at airports in large coastal cities. The number of cases did not go back to zero as Trump promised.

I was working with some people from California to organize fundraising events for the Democratic Party of Wisconsin. A few of them flew to Wisconsin to meet with us. I met them at the front door, shook their hands, and spoke with them face to face for a few minutes before taking them to meet with other people at the state party headquarters. They didn't look sick. I still don't know if they were.

A few days later, some people in the office started getting sick. I did not feel well. I had no appetite. I no longer had my sense of taste or smell. I was having trouble breathing which reminded me of my younger years when I dealt with asthma attacks. Many of us in the office felt terrible, but we all continued to work very hard in close proximity to each other. We didn't know what COVID was yet. We thought we had bad head colds. We had a million things to do. We were too busy to be sick. We were trying to change the course of history by kicking Donald Trump out of the White House.

A few weeks later, I was still not feeling well. My parents were planning a visit the following week. I wasn't sure if they should come. I told them they shouldn't visit until I felt better. I still had no idea I had COVID. Tests were not widely available yet. My parents were both in the age range that was dying from COVID. There's a chance that telling my parents to stay home might have saved the lives of one or both of them.

As COVID cases and hospitalizations started to rise, more people took precautions to avoid the virus. Many events were canceled. Society was shutting down as we all took cover in our homes. I was concerned about the rest of my family catching the virus.

We still had a lot of work to do, but we were now working from home. We used the video service Zoom to meet with each other. It was weird to work from home but also awesome. I no longer had to wait for a bus while the Wisconsin winters slapped me in the face. I no longer had to share an office with multiple people. I had my own kitchen and bathroom. These were the best working conditions I had ever experienced.

We were preparing for the spring 2020 elections in Wisconsin. There was an important State Supreme Court race we needed to win. We couldn't win the majority of seats on the court before the 2020 presidential election, but having another liberal justice on the State Supreme Court would be helpful in case there were challenges to the 2020 presidential election.

We spent a lot of time and money building neighborhood volunteer teams throughout the state. We were trying to activate them for the spring election and then keep them active for the presidential election in the fall. The goal was to have volunteers all over the state knocking on doors and making phone calls all year. Donald Trump won Wisconsin in 2016 by a very small margin. We hoped our neighborhood volunteer teams could make a difference if the fall election was close again.

COVID grounded the neighborhood volunteer teams. They were all stuck at home. We threw our plans out the window and started to adapt to the new situation. We turned our focus to phone calls and texting. Our new goal was to help people vote with absentee ballots from home.

Since there was a global pandemic going on, we wanted the state of Wisconsin to send an absentee ballot to every voter. This would be the safest option. Election day poll workers were often older people. During the first few months of the pandemic, mostly older people were dying. Having a bunch of older election poll workers face to face with voters did not seem like a good idea during a global pandemic caused by an airborne virus.

Wisconsin Republicans opposed the plan to send absentee ballots to all registered voters. They agreed with President Trump's view that the virus wasn't a big deal. Republicans also knew they would likely lose the election if more people voted.

Democrats were listening to the scientists. We saw daily cases, hospitalizations, and deaths rising. The virus was no joke. A lot of people were dying. The Democratic Party of Wisconsin had no intention of encouraging people to risk their safety to vote. We quickly became experts on how to request and return absentee ballots for the spring election. We set up a voter protection hotline to answer questions.

We found there was an unexpected benefit to using absentee ballots. The state generated reports of who had already voted through an absentee ballot. Once someone voted, we crossed them off our voter contact list so our volunteers would only call people who hadn't voted yet. The absentee ballot report also listed if there was an error with the ballot. We would contact the voter to let them know there was a problem with their ballot and how to fix it. The lists were available to both parties, but Republicans were encouraging their supporters to vote in person on election day during a global pandemic. It was a major error by Republicans.

The 2020 spring election in Wisconsin was a mess on election day. The Republican state assembly leader was captured on video in full medical protective gear and safety goggles at a polling location. He looked into the camera and said there was nothing to worry about. Why was he wearing full protective gear if there was nothing to worry about?

A lot of older election workers didn't show up on election day. They didn't want to risk their lives by working at polling locations. Many of these election workers were in democratic areas where people knew the virus was a real threat. A lot of polling locations had to be closed. Large democratic areas like Milwaukee only had a handful of polling locations open. The election day lines were very long. Most people were wearing masks and protective gear. It looked like some sort of apocalyptic scene from a movie. Someone waiting in line to vote was holding a sign that said, "This is ridiculous!"

It was a good thing we encouraged Democrats to vote by mail. We figured election day would be a mess, and it was. Many older conservative voters decided to stay home. Republicans made a huge mistake by turning their voters against absentee ballots during a global pandemic.

Not only did we win the spring elections, but we had a blueprint for how to win the presidential election if the virus lasted into the fall. I thought the pandemic would be over within a few weeks. I was still making plans for the state and national conventions later that summer. I had no idea the pandemic would continue throughout the 2020 campaign.

CHAPTER 21

2020 PRESIDENTIAL ELECTION

I worked and volunteered a lot during the 2018 campaign to defeat Republican Governor Scott Walker. Then I started managing all the fundraising efforts for the Democratic Party of Wisconsin. Then we got hit by a global pandemic. I had no time to rest or process what was happening. I was doing everything I could to ensure Donald Trump would lose Wisconsin. With only a few months left until the 2020 presidential election, there was so much work to do. Polls said the election was close and would probably come down to who won Wisconsin. We all felt the pressure.

The state and national conventions changed to virtual events due to the pandemic. I was bummed to miss my first national political convention, but I was proud of my fellow Democrats for following science and keeping people safe. I was also relieved because the cancellation of in-person conventions allowed me to cross a million things off my convention task lists.

Former Vice President Joe Biden was the 2020 Democratic candidate for president. The primary elections were very similar to the 2016 primary elections. The first few primaries were close. Then Biden won huge delegate totals in southern states on Super Tuesday, which put him on the path to being the Democratic nominee against President Donald Trump.

President Trump knew he was in trouble. The COVID virus was a threat to his presidency. The virus was a threat to the strong economy President Obama handed him. The United States had the longest streak of job growth in history, from about 2009 to 2020. Most of the job growth happened while President Obama was in office. Under Trump, job growth slowed as overall economic numbers stayed about the same. That didn't stop Trump from bragging about the economy whenever he could. Trump wanted to take credit for the economy all the way to reelection, but the virus was messing up his plans.

Trump told Americans the virus would soon disappear "like a miracle." Trump got mad when scientists started giving fact-based press conferences about the pandemic. He forced the scientists to only give press conferences from the White House, with Trump serving as the moderator. Trump ended up taking over the press conferences.

Instead of getting accurate information from scientists, Americans were being told by Trump not to worry about the virus. President Trump said if people were worried, they should try some unproven drugs he recommended. He wasn't saying this while standing on a snake oil salesman's stand; he was saying these things while standing in the White House as the president of the United States. It was embarrassing.

To minimize the threat of the virus, President Trump would often attack or try to discredit scientists. Many of Trump's supporters also started to attack scientists. Some scientists ended up needing bodyguards. Conservative rejection of science continued throughout the pandemic with grave results for many conservatives. The miracle cures President Trump promoted were not effective.

When President Trump realized the virus was not going away, he needed someone else to blame. He started calling it the "China Virus," hoping to rile up his base to focus their fears and anger toward China. He riled them up so much there were reports of violent attacks against people of Asian descent all over the United States. When Trump heard about these attacks, he stopped saying "China Virus" for a short time but later started saying it again.

As President Trump downplayed the threat of the virus, he continued to hold large campaign rallies. Most of his supporters were not wearing masks. President Trump rarely wore a mask since he said it wouldn't look good on him. He said he couldn't imagine other great leaders wearing a mask (eye roll). Many Republicans opposed masks throughout the pandemic. After three thousand Americans died on 9/11, Republicans asked military families to fight and die in costly wars. As a million Americans were dying from an airborne virus, Republicans said wearing a mask was asking too much.

Unfortunately, some high-profile Trump supporters got sick after attending Trump rallies, and some of them died. Trump's campaign rallies during the 2020 election were different from his rallies in 2016. In 2016, the rallies were seen as proof of how much support Trump had, but now the rallies were seen by many as irresponsible gatherings during a global pandemic.

Trump's campaign was desperate to keep having huge rallies. They got really excited when a lot of people signed up to attend a rally in Tulsa, Oklahoma. The Trump campaign decided to rent an additional stage outside the large arena for people who could not get into the rally. On the way to Tulsa, the Trump campaign was so excited they asked the pilot to fly over the arena before landing at the airport. Instead of seeing a large crowd, they saw an outdoor stage with only a handful of people. It wasn't much different when they arrived at the arena. The large arena was mostly empty.

It turns out a bunch of young people on the social media site TikTok organized an effort to reserve free seats at the Trump campaign rally with no intention of going. Someone on TikTok had an idea that grew into a newsworthy event that embarrassed President Trump shortly before the 2020 election. That's the power of social media. Small ideas can develop into major events. A picture in the news later that night showed President Trump returning to the White House looking very dejected. It looked like he was going to lose the election.

Democrats were still listening to scientists and being careful. Democratic candidate Joe Biden held virtual rallies and organized events in large parking lots where people stayed in their cars. While Trump attacked scientists, Democrats were talking about access to doctors for all Americans. While Trump was using the phrase "China virus" to rile up his base, Joe Biden talked about how we could improve our economy for everyone. It was hard to believe people still supported President Trump. Couldn't they see he was a con man who hadn't done anything in four years to help Americans?

Whenever I needed to remind myself the election would be close, I would click on the conservative Twitter list I had created. I was shocked to see how excited they were to vote for President Trump. I was also surprised by the amount of misinformation they posted about COVID. I tried to engage with some of these conservative accounts, but few of them were willing to have a respectful debate.

I would ask the conservative accounts why Trump's healthcare or infrastructure plans were always "about two weeks" away, but nothing happened over four years. I asked why Trump's tax cut mostly helped the wealthy after Trump promised his tax cut wouldn't help the wealthy. I asked conservatives why the yearly deficits were now higher under Trump (even before COVID), but conservatives were silent. I asked if they lost their Tea Party protest voice or perhaps they had a bad case of hypocrisy. Some conservatives were willing to discuss the facts, but they would quickly run away or block my Twitter account as soon as they figured out they were losing the debate.

Trump channeled American anger, fear, and frustrations but delivered nothing in return. All we got was a deficit-spiking tax cut that mostly helped the wealthy. Blaming other people solved zero issues. "Drain the swamp" was just Trump's campaign propaganda since Republicans continue to block campaign finance reforms (and Trump hired one of the swampiest list of characters ever assembled).

I couldn't believe the election was as close as it was. I would not be able to handle another four years of Trump selling his daily dose of nonsense from the White House. I needed to raise more money to hire more field organizers to ensure we won Wisconsin.

CHAPTER 22

THE PRINCESS BRIDE CAST REUNION

Celebrities were a big part of our fundraising efforts during the 2020 presidential campaign. They wanted to be involved. They knew Wisconsin was a key swing state that could determine the outcome of the election. They were at home with lots of time on their hands. Most film and television productions were shut down due to the pandemic.

As we were learning how to host virtual conventions during the summer of 2020, we also learned how to host virtual fundraisers. We worked with Bradley Whitford to organize a reunion of *The West Wing* characters, Josh and Donna (Janel Moloney), on a podcast called *The West Wing Weekly*. We set it up so anyone who donated any amount to WisDems would get a link to watch the event. It was a great time with no technical difficulties! We raised more donations than we would have raised through a traditional in-person fundraising event. There were no donation envelopes to open! I didn't have to wear a tie!

In addition to the fundraising events, we asked celebrities to post fundraising links on social media during our end-of-month fundraising drives. They were more than willing to help. Other celebrities saw their posts and wanted to get involved too. The digital fundraising drives continued to break donation records. We used the money to hire more field organizers and voter protection lawyers.

One of the employees at WisDems was in contact with someone who knew the actor Cary Elwes. He played the lead character, Wesley, in the movie *The Princess Bride*. He mentioned something about putting together a movie cast reunion as a way to help defeat President Trump in Wisconsin. He said the movie's director, Rob Reiner, was also interested. Many of us loved the movie and were excited to organize an event.

Cary Elwes was one of the greatest people we worked with during the 2020 campaign. His character in the movie was a farm boy who said, "As you wish," whenever the woman he loved asked him to do something. He basically said the same thing to us whenever we asked him to do something. He would contact other celebrities and post event links on his social media accounts. In the movie, he fought a character named Humperdinck, but on social media, he posted about defeating #Trumperdinck.

Most of the original cast members were excited to join the event. Robin Wright was available to play her role as Princess Buttercup. Mandy Patinkin was excited to help with his classic line, "Hello. My name is Inigo Montoya. You killed my father. Prepare to die." I used to watch the Comic Relief charity specials with Robin Williams, Whoopi Goldberg, and Billy Crystal, so I was really excited to hear Billy Crystal had agreed to join the event to play his character, Miracle Max.

Andre the Giant died in 1993, so Josh Gad agreed to play the role of Fezzik. I wasn't sure who Josh Gad was, but since I was a stay-at-home dad for many years, I knew him all too well after learning he was the voice of the snowman, Olaf, in the movie *Frozen*. Fred Savage was a conservative (and too old to play the grandson laying in bed), so we were happy to hear Finn Wolfhard from the Netflix series *Stranger Things* was joining the event.

When we announced *The Princess Bride* reunion, people were really excited. It would be the first time the cast gathered to read the movie script in many years. Donations started rolling in. We asked our celebrity contacts to post the event link on social media. We started to get coverage on entertainment news websites. Some of the articles included a link to our ActBlue event donation page.

Then it happened. Republican Senator Ted Cruz was not happy about the cast of his favorite movie, *The Princess Bride*, doing a fundraiser for WisDems. He was jealous and complained about it during an interview. His comments about the fundraiser led to a front-page article on CNN's website. The article included our event link! CNN later moved the article lower on the front page but kept it there for numerous days. It was a very popular article.

We were also having a lot of luck advertising the event on Facebook. We announced the cast lineup with advertising graphics that looked like baseball cards. Our Facebook advertising consultant tested and tweaked ads until a high conversion rate was found. Since we continued to generate more donations, we continued to buy more Facebook ads.

The night of the event was nerve-racking but really exciting. We weren't sure if our technical systems could handle a political rally of such unusual size (our own R.O.U.S.). Around 100,000 people logged into the event, and everything seemed stable. The cast read the entire script and enjoyed a great conversation. Billy Crystal was in his Miracle Max outfit with original movie props hanging on the wall behind him. A great last-minute addition to the event was executive producer Norman Lear.

The Princess Bride reunion event generated $4.25 million for the Democratic Party of Wisconsin! That was close to our entire yearly budget a few years earlier. Not only did we raise that much money, but we also now had the contact information of ActBlue donors all over the country. We continued to stay in touch with those donors as we got closer to the election. Many of them attended other fundraising events and donated through the email fundraising program.

Since we were setting fundraising records, we decided to do as many digital events as possible. Celebrities saw the success of *The Princess Bride* reunion and wanted to get involved. We did a *VEEP* reunion with Julia Louis-Dreyfus. We put together a *Rocky Horror Picture Show* Halloween event with Tim Curry. We had a *Parks and Recreation* event with Amy Poehler, Adam Scott, Aubrey Plaza, Retta, Nick Offerman, Jim O'Heir, and Michael Schur. We had a hilarious *Superbad* movie night watch party with Jonah Hill, Seth Rogen, Emma Stone, Michael Cera, Christopher Mintz-Plasse, Bill Hader, Martha MacIsaac, Evan Goldberg, Greg Mottola, and Judd Apatow. Since we were in Wisconsin, we thought it was fitting to have a *Happy Days* reunion with The Fonz (Henry Winkler), Richie Cunningham (Ron Howard), and other cast members.

I really enjoyed being a part of so many great fundraising events. A group of about eight of us put the shows together. We sometimes felt like we were a Hollywood production studio rather than a political organization. We saw the field team growing each month, so it motivated us to keep putting in the long hours necessary to put on so many digital fundraising events.

In addition to working on the fundraising shows, I was still managing the direct mail program and the email fundraising list. Direct mail could be done during the day, but the best time to send an email was when people were leaving work. I watched the email stats to see which test version did the best and then decided whether or not to send the winning email version to a larger segment of the email list. I watched the statistics late into the night to ensure there were no problems with the email or the ActBlue donation page.

As I watched fundraising email statistics, I often posted donation links with my Twitter accounts. My wife once asked me why I was still working at 10 p.m. I told her I was posting donation links on Twitter because it was prime time for California donors, and we needed to hire more field organizers to defeat Trump.

I was always looking for crazy quotes from President Trump to use in the email fundraising program. They were not hard to find. People on our email list were more likely to open the message and send a donation if we were the first ones to tell them what Trump said. This meant I needed to keep track of what President Trump was saying and get emails out as quickly as possible. It was exhausting.

There were times when I thought I would not make it to the 2020 election. I was tired and needed a break. No break time was available in 2020. Sure, I had vacation time I hadn't used, and sick time I could use, but there was no way I had time to step away. I was doing everything I could to make sure President Trump would lose Wisconsin.

I was also losing track of my home life and quality time with my kids. Even when we found time on weekends to do something, I was often on my phone approving fundraising emails or posting donation links on social media. My family encouraged me to keep doing everything I could to defeat Trump. There was no way I was going to quit. There was no way I was going to let Donald Trump win Wisconsin.

As we entered the campaign's final month, the state party's leadership announced there would be no more weekends off. We were expected to work around the clock, seven days per week. I was not ready for this. I was just as dedicated as anyone else, but I was already near collapse after many years of stressful working conditions. I was going to make sure we defeated Donald Trump, but I also started thinking about getting out of politics as I crawled my way to the election day finish line.

I didn't think I needed to see a therapist, but in reality, the campaign was killing me physically and mentally. I was gaining weight and dealing with a lot of stress. Our medical plan fully covered online therapy sessions, so I figured it couldn't hurt.

I didn't go into any great details with the therapist. My main goal was to make it through the last four weeks of the campaign. She gave me strategies for dealing with stress. I promised to stop "rewarding" myself with trips to fast food drive-through windows. I was really glad I scheduled the therapy sessions. They helped me put things into perspective while keeping me accountable for my weight loss goals.

Did I still want this stressful job after the election? I enjoyed working in politics, but managing the email fundraising program for the past three years was too stressful and time-consuming. Each Thanksgiving, I needed to prepare the end-of-month emails. Each Christmas, I needed to prepare end-of-year emails. Being part of the rapid response team at WisDems meant I was always working.

I told the state party I wanted to train someone else to manage the email fundraising program after the election. I wanted to spend time working on the WisDems website along with creating a streaming channel for the party. I wasn't sure what my future would hold, but I needed to stop managing the email fundraising program. Three years of rapid response duties had taken a toll on me.

Shortly before the election, the leadership of the state party said all employees would need to reapply for our jobs. We knew the party would need to lay off a lot of people after the election, but even senior staff members were no longer guaranteed a job. If we all needed to reapply for the same jobs, then maybe I shouldn't have told them I no longer wanted to manage the email program.

I could apply for other jobs at the state party, but there were already people in those jobs who would reapply for them. I doubted they would be able to create a new position for me to work on other digital projects. They would need my salary to pay a new person to manage the email program.

About two weeks before the election, I realized I would probably lose my job. I was trying to do everything I could to defeat President Trump while also acknowledging my family was about to be thrown out into the cold during a global pandemic. I really needed a break, but instead of being able to rest after the election, I would be looking for a new job before my son's asthma medicine ran out.

CHAPTER 23

COUP COUP BANANAS

Before the 2020 election, President Trump attacked Democrats for voting through the mail with absentee ballots. Most of the polls showed Biden was expected to win the election, but Trump said the only way he would lose was if Democrats cheated. Journalists asked President Trump if he would support a peaceful transition of power, but Trump said he would wait to see if he won or lost.

Since the global pandemic was still killing a lot of people, a large number of people voted safely from home with absentee ballots in 2020. Political organizations started running television ads telling people it might take a few days to count the ballots and declare an election winner. I remembered how the absentee ballots in Milwaukee County were reported late into the night during the 2018 election for governor. I thought it might be a day or two for Milwaukee to process a much larger number of absentee ballots during the 2020 presidential election.

After the polls closed on election day, it still looked like Wisconsin would determine the outcome of the election. I really hoped we did enough to win. We were all so exhausted I don't think we could have done any more. President Trump took a huge lead in Wisconsin as the in-person vote was counted and reported first. It was very late into the night when Milwaukee County finished counting the absentee ballots. As required by Wisconsin law, they waited until all absentee ballots were counted and then reported the numbers at once.

The next day, Trump claimed there was fraud happening in Wisconsin. Trump posted on social media, "Last night I was leading, often solidly, in many key States, in almost all instances Democrat run & controlled. Then, one by one, they started to magically disappear as surprise ballot dumps were counted. VERY STRANGE, and the 'pollsters' got it completely & historically wrong!"

There were no "surprise ballot dumps" in swing states. Election officials, campaign workers, and journalists knew the absentee ballots would be reported once the counting was done. The Trump campaign either expected us to believe they didn't know how votes were reported, or they were being way too obvious with their lies about the election.

I knew Trump was lying. Trump's campaign knew Wisconsin law requires absentee ballots to be reported after they are all counted. Trump knew this, but he continued to claim the vote was fraudulent. I couldn't believe the president of the United States was lying about election results. This was the first time I thought Trump might be attempting a coup to stay in power. He was whipping up his supporters with obvious lies. Trump supporters created a "Stop the Steal" movement. They were sure the election was stolen, but they didn't have any evidence.

In Antrim County, Michigan, thousands of votes for President Trump were accidentally credited to Joe Biden. The Republican election officials reported and corrected the error the morning after the election while explaining it was a human clerical error. Trump cronies flew a private jet to the county to demand an inspection of the voting machines used in the county. Even though local officials told the Trump team it was a human clerical error that had been corrected, the Trump campaign pushed a false narrative about voting machines being rigged.

After many days of vote counting in swing states, Joe Biden was declared the winner of the election. Joe Biden won swing state Wisconsin by a little over twenty thousand votes out of over three million votes cast in the state. It was another close election in Wisconsin where everything we did made a difference. *The Princess Bride* cast reunion probably won the 2020 presidential election since it allowed WisDems to hire so many field organizers.

Joe Biden also won very close elections in Arizona and Georgia, which gave him the Electoral College victory. Joe Biden won the national popular vote by more than seven million votes out of 158 million votes cast. However, Biden only won the Electoral College by about forty thousand votes spread throughout Arizona, Georgia, and Wisconsin. Trump almost won a second term. The election was much closer than most people realize—a difference of 40,000 votes out of 158,000,000 votes cast.

Trump and his campaign continued to spread conspiracy theories about rigged voting machines and massive levels of voter fraud. None of the claims were true. The story about a suitcase full of ballots in Georgia went viral on right-wing media. Republican officials in Georgia gave a lengthy presentation showing there was no fraud involved. President Trump attacked the Republican governor and secretary of state in Georgia for not "finding" an extra 11,780 votes needed for him to win the state.

In addition to losing the presidency, Republicans were also close to losing control of the U.S. Senate. Georgia has a law that says candidates must win at least fifty percent of the vote to take office. Otherwise, there is a runoff election with the two highest vote-getters squaring off. There were two U.S. Senate elections in 2020 in Georgia, and both went to runoff elections. If Democrats won both runoff elections, they would win control of the U.S. Senate. The Senate runoff elections were scheduled two months after the presidential election on January 5, 2021.

Soon-to-be former President Trump was still really mad about losing the election. He told voters it wasn't worth voting because he believed the election was so fraudulent. This led to lower voter turnout among Georgia Republicans on January 5, allowing both Democrats to win the Senate runoff elections. Trump was so obsessed with staying in power that his complaints ended up giving Democrats control of the U.S. Senate.

The claims of fraud in Georgia were repeatedly proven false by Republican election officials. Trump's team of lawyers tried to overturn elections in many states, but it was often Trump-appointed judges who rejected the claims. In Wisconsin, Trump decided to pay for a recount of the two largest counties, but the recount confirmed Joe Biden won Wisconsin.

The Trump team organized a large rally in Washington, D.C., for January 6, 2021. It was the same day Congress would certify Joe Biden's victory in the Electoral College. Trump's supporters organized efforts to storm the nation's Capitol and stop the certification process. President Trump claimed Vice President Mike Pence had the power to stop the certification process, but Pence rejected the president's claim. Since Pence said he would not stop the certification process, some of Trump's supporters believed they needed to stop the certification process with violence. They broke into the Capitol while chanting, "Hang Mike Pence!" They wanted to kill the vice president of the United States to stop the certification of Joe Biden as president. Their actions were based on election lies pushed by President Trump.

The attempted coup on January 6 made me feel like I was living in some sort of banana republic where autocratic leaders ignore the will of the people. I couldn't believe so many Republicans believed the election lies. This wasn't just some fringe far-right movement. Polls showed nearly two-thirds of Republicans believed Donald Trump had won the election. My country had somehow gone coup coup bananas.

Thankfully, the coup attempt was unsuccessful. After the Capitol was cleared of insurrectionists, Joe Biden was certified as the election winner. President Trump was directly responsible for the attack on the Capitol. He was the leader who spread election lies while encouraging his supporters to fight like hell for their country.

Democrats immediately started a process to impeach President Trump. This was the second time President Trump was impeached. He was impeached the first time for using taxpayer-funded military assistance to extort the president of Ukraine. He was impeached the second time for inciting a violent coup attempt at the Capitol. President Trump was impeached in the House of Representatives both times but was saved by Republicans in the U.S. Senate. They blocked the conviction and removal of President Trump both times.

President Trump never conceded the 2020 election. He didn't show up to welcome Joe Biden to the White House, a first for an outgoing president. The former president continued to spread election lies with no evidence to back up his claims. Lots of Republicans still believed his election lies.

A few weeks later, Republicans in Arizona hired a group called the Cyber Ninjas to audit the election in the largest county of Arizona. Trump supporters were certain the audit would discover massive levels of fraud that would overturn the election. The final report from the Cyber Ninjas confirmed Joe Biden won the election. However, the report also said they found 74,000 more ballots than expected. Election officials in Arizona quickly explained to the Cyber Ninjas they had made a mistake. The Cyber Ninjas agreed they made an error, and the 74,000 ballots were accounted for. Later that night, former President Trump held a campaign rally. He didn't say anything about Joe Biden being confirmed as the winner of the election. He told his supporters the audit found 74,000 fraudulent ballots. He knew he was lying.

I wasn't surprised Trump continued to push election lies, but I was very surprised so many Republicans believed the lies. Republicans spent decades waving their pocket Constitutions at us. Now they ignored the Constitution by demanding the election be overturned without evidence. False right-wing memes shared by conservatives on Facebook and Twitter were not "evidence" capable of overturning an election. The Constitution is very clear about this.

During the investigation into the January 6 coup attempt, it was incredible to discover how much planning went into the insurrection. Lots of Trump supporters were just there for the rally, but specific people had specific plans for that day. Senior members of the Trump team used burner phones to hide their messages. Right-wing militias made plans to capture or kill Vice President Pence and Speaker Pelosi. President Trump remained silent for hours during the attack on the Capitol. When he finally broke his silence, he tried to justify the attack on the Capitol by saying, "We had an election that was stolen from us."

The election was not stolen. Joe Biden won. America won. The world won. The election was won by thousands of campaign workers, like myself, who put everything we had into removing a con man and sexual abuser from the White House. The election was won by people who support science and the truth. It felt like the campaign never ended. We were still fighting Trump's lies. I didn't get much of a break after the election.

CHAPTER 24

TRANSITION TIME

I was looking forward to getting some rest after election day, but the election drama kept all of us busy. We expected a recount in Wisconsin along with legal challenges. I prepared daily fundraising emails to make sure we could afford to hire election lawyers to monitor the recount and court cases.

I was still working after the election, but I was also in a state of shock that I needed to look for a new job. Some WisDems employees were already being laid off. Field organizers were sending emails saying goodbye. A coworker got a job in Georgia setting up a digital fundraising event with the cast of the Broadway musical *Hamilton*. They were raising money for the Democratic Senate candidates in the Georgia runoff elections.

My employment was extended a couple of months until January 15, 2021. They needed me to keep raising money for the recount and election challenges. I didn't know most of the people who were making decisions about my future. In the past, we were a tight-knit group that worked together in the WisDems office. During the pandemic, many of my former coworkers had left the state party and were replaced with campaign workers from around the country working through Zoom. Some people making the employment decisions at WisDems had never stepped foot in Wisconsin and had no plans to move to Wisconsin after the pandemic. I had worked at the state party longer than anyone else in the organization, but I had only worked there for four years. Nobody lasted very long in these types of jobs.

A few months earlier, my wife asked what I would do if I left the stressful world of political campaigns. I enjoyed working on my business websites and had participated in a few events organized by the Madison business community. I told my wife I wanted to work for a technology start-up company in Madison, but at the time, I figured I would stay in politics for a few more years. Now I found myself looking for and applying to any job I could find.

I was exhausted and stressed about losing my job and health insurance during a global pandemic. I didn't tell my kids. They had enough to worry about while navigating their journey through at-home schooling. Telling them we might be kicked off our health insurance would be extra stress they didn't need. My wife and I didn't need the stress either, but we dealt with it the best we could.

The first job listing I applied to was a security guard position at the University of Wisconsin Hospital. The job was not what I was looking for, but it was available and offered my family health insurance. One reason the job was available was that very few people wanted a job at a hospital during a pandemic. Security guards were responsible for moving the bodies of dead patients from the COVID wing to the morgue. I was willing to do it to ensure my family had health insurance, but it was not the job I wanted. I decided to cancel the second interview.

A job I was excited about was with one of the best start-up technology companies in Madison. The main downside was the job was with the field sales team, which included a lot of travel. I already missed my kids after spending so much time working in politics for the past four years. I didn't pursue the field sales job. I continued looking for other jobs, but I wasn't finding much. My job search slowed to a crawl as employers took breaks for the Thanksgiving, Christmas, and New Year holidays. I was about a month away from losing my income and healthcare. It was a stressful holiday season during a global pandemic.

I knew I was not alone. There were campaign workers all over the country in similar situations. Not all of them had families to support, but we were all recently laid off after putting everything we had into a campaign. Lots of the messages I saw on social media commented about how quiet everything seemed after months of being surrounded by campaign buzz. Most political campaigns wouldn't start for another year, so campaign workers often need to spend time doing something else until the next election season begins. I was now a few weeks away from needing to pay for very expensive health insurance without the help of an employer plan.

Former coworkers, who had also been laid off, were sending me job listings for spring election campaign jobs. Big city mayor candidates were already hiring, but I didn't want to move my family to a new state. I looked for jobs with nonprofit organizations, but most of them were in Washington, D.C., or New York. I applied with a local Goodwill store to be in charge of taking pictures for their online store, but I didn't get the job.

I didn't pursue the field sales job at the Madison tech company because I didn't want to leave the kids for two weeks at a time. However, I was very happy when I received an email saying they now had an inside sales job I could apply for. I applied for the job, went through the interview process, and was hired just a few days before my health insurance with WisDems ended. It was a stressful time, but I was lucky to get a new job lined up just in time to avoid losing health insurance.

During my first week at the technology company, I worked from home and shut my computer off at 5 p.m. I said hello to my kids and told them I was done with work. They looked at me with disbelief and asked if I was really done. It was a great feeling for all of us to realize I had no work responsibilities until the next morning. The following weekend was the first in many years when I was not working or looking for a job. It was wonderful to work a normal job with normal hours without the pressure of the world resting on my shoulders.

I wasn't sure how long I would stay at the technology company. There was a chance I would get back into politics to help defeat U.S. Senator Ron Johnson in the 2022 elections. The health insurance plan at my new job was not the same plan I had at WisDems. Did I really want to get to know a new doctor if I might be switching healthcare plans again within a few months? I ended up staying at the technology company. I waited over a year to make medical appointments for myself, which was way too long. This reminded me it is a really bad idea, as a country, to have our healthcare plans tied to our employers.

CHAPTER 25

PRESIDENT JOE BIDEN

It was great to see Joe Biden inaugurated as the president of the United States. Donald Trump was still crying and lying but no longer in power. President Biden was respectful. He was dedicated to getting the country moving again. The White House was no longer the source of unproven drug recommendations and crass insults. Lots of us started to breathe easier.

The country was a mess when President Biden took office. It was just like when Republican President George W. Bush handed President Obama a total mess. Both democratic presidents went to work and fixed many of the problems given to them. Republicans ignored the progress as they blamed the mess on Democrats.

Life was returning to normal, but it takes time for everything to return to normal after economic disruptions. During the pandemic, very few people were driving or traveling. Demand for gas was very low which led to very low gas prices. Oil companies laid off truck drivers and drillers. As people started driving again, demand for gas rose faster than oil companies could rehire and train truckers and drillers. In a market-based economy, prices increase when demand rises faster than supply. The same price inflation was happening in many industries. We saw similar inflation worldwide as economies quickly recovered from the pandemic.

The good news was that companies started hiring millions of people to meet the surging demand for products and services. Millions of jobs were added back to the economy. Additional waves of COVID continued to sweep around the world, but death rates were lower as more people were vaccinated. Most people figured prices would come back down once the supply chains were back to normal unless there was a war or something like that.

I finally had a chance to reflect on the prior few years and how crazy it all was. I ended up being in the right place at the right time to help make a difference. It felt great when Republican Governor Scott Walker was no longer in office, but it felt like I helped save the world when Donald Trump was no longer our president. Who we elect to power makes a difference. We all have the power to determine who gets elected. We all have the power to vote, volunteer, and donate. We all have the ability to make a difference in our own unique ways.

I found myself smiling again. My dreams came true. I started working at the Democratic Party of Wisconsin feeling like I was in the "room where it happened," but l left WisDems knowing I made a difference in the Zoom where it happened. I had the same relaxed feeling I had after President Obama was elected. Yes, the Democratic presidents were put in very difficult situations when they took office, but I could see better decisions being made with better results. The differences were noticeable as soon as Democrats took power.

The first thing Democrats did in Congress was to pass campaign finance reforms through the House of Representatives. Unfortunately, Republicans in the Senate once again blocked campaign finance reforms. Since campaign finance reforms don't impact the budget, it requires sixty votes in the hundred-member U.S. Senate to be passed. Republicans didn't offer compromises or their own proposals. They didn't want to talk about campaign finance reforms. They simply blocked reforms as wealthy donors cheered and sent them more campaign cash.

Democrats used the fifty-vote budget process in the Senate to strengthen assistance programs for Americans. They also ramped up COVID vaccine production and distribution. Former President Trump should have bragged about how the vaccine was created while he was president, but conservatives had turned against science. Many of them had also turned against the vaccine. When Trump tried to promote the vaccine at one of his rallies, the crowd booed him. Conservatives were pushing false claims as they misled each other, literally to death. COVID death percentages in counties Trump won were higher than in counties won by President Biden.

President Trump bragged about how he was a "builder" who could restore American greatness "very easily" with great infrastructure deals to build bridges, airports, and seaports. Unfortunately, Donald Trump was lying again. He failed to invest in American infrastructure during his four years in office. President Biden signed an infrastructure bill within ten months of taking office. I was very happy to see infrastructure investments finally being made in America again.

President Biden pledged to lead by example by getting the United States back into the Paris Climate Accords. Some Republicans say other countries are cheating as they produce a lot of pollution, so we should cheat too, but this is a criminal argument. America should lead the world through our example. We should continue striving to create sustainable energy sources that will power life on Earth for future generations. As technology continues to improve, sustainable forms of energy are becoming more affordable than burning fossil fuels.

I'm happy to see President Biden and Democrats promoting workers' rights. President Biden often said during the campaign he wanted to be the most pro-union president leading the most pro-union administration in history. Workers benefited from the improvements in the American Rescue Plan and the infrastructure investments. Union member Marty Walsh was appointed to be the secretary of labor. Anti-labor members of the National Labor Relations Board (NLRB) appointed by President Trump were replaced with Biden appointees who supported workers' rights.

Since most of our problems are related to poverty, I was happy to see President Biden and the Democrats reduce poverty by expanding the childhood tax credit. The program sent money each month to families with children. It lifted a lot of families out of poverty. Families spent the money on rent, groceries, childcare, and education. Then, Republicans in the Senate voted to end the program.

Republicans call themselves "pro-life" as they kick families off anti-poverty programs. I grew up in the Catholic Church (and Catholic schools for a few years), so everyone around me was pro-life. How could you not support babies? As I grew older, I learned about things like rape, incest, medical complications, and personal choices. I'm now pro-choice, but my personal choice is life whenever possible. I found there are great ways to reduce the number of abortions. Studies show abortions are less likely to happen if we reduce poverty levels and increase access to healthcare. Republicans are not being pro-life when they cut successful anti-poverty programs and restrict access to healthcare options such as Medicaid. Since I don't agree with completely banning abortion, the best way for me to reduce the number of abortions is to vote for Democrats.

Since Republicans claim to be pro-life, I asked them on social media if they were happy about millions of families being lifted out of poverty by the expanded childhood tax credit. A few acknowledged the good news but said they don't like their tax money assisting other people. I told them keeping people out of poverty costs less tax money than policing and jailing people. It is similar to how taxpayer money spent on foreign diplomacy and global assistance programs helps avoid much costlier wars. While some conservatives opposed all government programs, most of the conservatives said the poverty reduction was just "fake news" from Democrats. President Trump taught his followers to yell "fake news" whenever they need to ignore facts.

It didn't surprise me that Republicans ignored President Biden's accomplishments. It was the same way after President Obama took office. Republicans screamed about the national debt and the destruction of America but forgot to cheer when President Obama decreased yearly deficits and saved the American economy with the longest streak of job growth in history. Republicans said President Obama's Affordable Care Act would destroy America, but the country was not destroyed. The healthcare reforms allowed people to get preventative care instead of showing up at the emergency room with expensive problems. Lots of people now support the Affordable Care Act. Most of us also agree government programs such as Social Security and Medicare have greatly reduced poverty among senior citizens.

Republicans should be happy with job growth and the reduction of yearly budget deficits under Democratic presidents, but they still scream about America being destroyed. The same type of "team bias" happens in sports when we rarely think our team committed a foul while thinking the other team is always committing fouls. The same thing happens in global affairs when we cheer for invasions done by our country but oppose the invasions done by other countries.

Regarding war and peace, I was relieved President Trump didn't invade any countries, but I was not a fan of his foreign policy. He greatly increased the number of drone strikes around the world while removing safeguards designed to limit civilian casualties. He helped dictators by saying torture is sometimes necessary. He used taxpayer-funded military equipment as a bargaining chip to get personal favors from foreign leaders.

Donald Trump taunted the leader of North Korea with the nickname "Rocket Man," which was unnecessary and irresponsible. The only sense I could make of it was if both leaders secretly agreed to taunt each other for a few months so they could brag about a diplomatic "breakthrough" when they met with each other. They both used images of themselves meeting on the border between North and South Korea to whip up support at home. Nothing of significance was accomplished other than a photo opportunity. Trump helped a brutal, nuclear-armed dictator present himself as a legitimate leader on the global stage.

I was not a fan of Trump leaving the nuclear deal with Iran. It is a tough situation, but we have two choices: Find a diplomatic solution to stop Iran from creating a nuclear weapon, or we go to war since we have a policy that says a nuclear weapon in Iran is unacceptable. The deal with Iran made by President Obama was working. When

President Trump ripped up the Iran deal, it put us back on the path to another costly war.

President Trump seemed jealous of the power dictators have. He tended to praise dictators while attacking the leaders of democratic countries. There were even reports of President Trump asking military leaders if he could order the military to shoot American citizens protesting him! He had no respect for our democratic republic and no respect for our Constitution. The fact-free election lies pushed by Donald Trump was something a dictator would do.

The audits, recounts, and court cases all said President Joe Biden won the 2020 presidential election. I'm so happy we worked as hard as we did to elect a president who respects American democracy and our democratic allies around the world. Who we elect to power makes a huge difference in so many ways. We live in a democratic republic, which is why we were able to get rid of Donald Trump. Millions of us played a role in that effort. Millions of us made a difference in our own unique ways.

CHAPTER 26

PUTIN'S WAR CRIMES

I'm spending my nights and weekends writing a book about peace. Then a huge war breaks out in Europe. The dictator in Russia, Vladimir Putin, has been bombing and terrorizing the people of Ukraine. There have been other wars in Yemen, Syria, Ethiopia, and a few other places. Still, Ukraine borders American allies in Europe, so the war has been getting a lot of news coverage in the United States.

After seeing news about the war, my wife and I talked about Putin's invasion of Ukraine. I told her about kids in Ukraine calling out for their deceased parents after bombings. We both started to tear up. We couldn't imagine our kids going through the violence of war. Watching the news about the war reminded me why I'm writing a book about peace.

Once a war begins, soldiers start shooting hot lead and chemicals at each other, with civilians caught in the crossfire. Most soldiers on both sides would rather be at home with their families. Why do we do such stupid things? Far too often, the ego and greed of old men in power mislead us into brutal wars.

Russia's leader, Vladimir Putin, wanted to reclaim the glory of the old Soviet empire. He claimed he must protect Russia from foreign nations and foreign cultures. Putin is an old man with old ideas. Dictators often claim to support their nation, but they mostly just steal the nation's wealth as they mislead, imprison, and impoverish most of the population.

After building up troops for many months, Russia claimed it had no intention of attacking Ukraine. Some military analysts wondered if Putin was waiting for the 2022 Winter Olympics in China to end before starting the invasion. What a stark contrast it was to see the world gathered together peacefully as a dictator was building up military forces to bomb civilian areas in Ukraine. A few days after the Olympics ended, Putin ordered the Russian military to invade Ukraine.

Ukraine has every right to align itself with the democratic republics of Europe. The people of Ukraine voted in favor of agreements with the European Union, but the Ukrainian leader at that time was a Russian puppet who rejected agreements with Europe. The Ukrainian people protested Putin's puppet leader and elected new leaders. As Putin saw Ukraine slipping away from his control in 2014, he invaded and occupied Eastern areas of Ukraine along with the Crimean peninsula, which is part of Ukraine. Putin greatly expanded his invasion of Ukraine in 2022. People in Ukraine were voting to leave Putin's grip, but Putin wasn't willing to let go.

Since Russian media is heavily censored, I was trying to send information about the war to people living in Russia. Online activists posted information about Putin's war on Russian websites, but most of it would get censored. We found some success posting information within reviews for Russian restaurants, museums, and hotels. I also responded to Twitter posts from Russia Today (RT) and other Russian state media outlets. Putin's supporters said I was a hypocrite for being an American who criticized Russia's invasion. However, since I opposed all invasions, I reminded them they were the only hypocrites for opposing invasions except for Russian invasions.

There were a lot of similarities between debating Putin supporters and Trump supporters. They were sure they were correct even though they had no evidence to support their claims. Vladimir Putin said reports from Ukraine were fake news that the Russian people should ignore. Putin said he was stopping a Nazi country, but the reality was Ukraine had recently elected a Jewish president and has a smaller number of right-wing groups than most other countries. Russians and Ukrainians fought together to defend their homes from the Nazi army in the 1940s, but now Russia was invading and killing their neighbors.

Putin wanted to blame the war on Ukraine, but American intelligence officials showed the world how Putin built up forces for months on the borders of Ukraine. After Putin ordered the Russian troops to invade, Ukrainian military forces fought back and decimated the Russian military in numerous battles. Putin thought his troops would easily conquer the Ukrainian capital city, Kyiv, but Russian troops were defeated on the outskirts of Kyiv and never entered the capital city.

As Donald Trump was calling Putin a "genius" for his "savvy" invasion of Ukraine, President Joe Biden worked to keep our democratic allies united within the North Atlantic Treaty Organization (NATO). Biden's plan was to support Ukraine while avoiding direct conflict, and a wider war, with Russia. Since an old, corrupt dictator in Russia was invading other countries, Sweden and Finland decided to join NATO.

Putin supporters declared him a master strategist, but Putin ended up strengthening the NATO alliance while destroying his military, economy, and credibility.

I have the freedom to oppose the leaders of my country, but Russians do not have the freedom to oppose Vladimir Putin or the war. As bad news was piling up, Russian media censorship was increasing. Putin's dictatorship said anyone reporting on the war or even using the term "war" would be jailed for ten to fifteen years. Russian media outlets were only allowed to use the phrase "special military operation" when discussing the war. The media censorship reminded me there are major differences between dictatorships and democratic republics. It reminded me to thank my lucky stars that I live in a democratic republic. It reminded me to do everything I can to strengthen and protect democratic republics.

Ukrainians were voting in large numbers to be more democratic. Russian elections were marred by opposition candidates being killed, poisoned, and imprisoned. Putin's invasion of Ukraine was a flashpoint in the global battle between democracies and dictatorships. Russia pretends to be a democracy, but Putin is a dictator committing war crimes.

CHAPTER 27

DEMOCRACY VS. DICTATORSHIP

Recently, democracies outnumbered dictatorships on Earth for the first time in history. However, these numbers are disputed since some democracies are not very democratic. We have also seen some democracies overthrown and returned to dictatorships. Hopefully, democracies will regain the lead and continue our progress toward a world without dictatorships.

Being at this tipping point in history should motivate all of us to support democracy. People all over the world want transparent and accountable forms of government. Most of us agree the best way to achieve our goals is through peace rather than war. We have the ability to pursue liberty and justice for all within peaceful communities of life.

We're solving some of our biggest problems. For example, we all need food and water to survive. To secure the resources we need, we have two choices: we can fight brutal wars, or we can figure out how to distribute resources without violence. We're solving this problem by using math-based market systems to trade with each other. We're now more likely to trade with each other rather than invade each other.

Trading with each other has reduced the number of wars we have fought over the past few centuries, but markets aren't perfect. Markets say kids living in poverty don't have enough value to see a doctor or go to school. Markets say it is very profitable for a business to get rid of toxic waste by dumping it into the river. While markets give us a universal system for trading with each other, market values are not the only values we should consider.

How do we decide which values will guide our decisions? Military dictatorships want everything based on military values. Religious dictatorships want everything based on religious values. Market dictatorships want everything based on market values.

To solve this problem, we created constitutional democratic republics. The goal is to consider all values as we make decisions in democratic ways. We still have a lot of improvements to make, but democratic forms of government are much better than dictatorships.

I'm not a fan of anarchists and libertarians who say we don't need governments. There are way too many of us on this planet to think we can just live our own separate lives. We need to have law and order, but who establishes law and order?

Having dictators establish law and order is a really bad idea. Nobody wants their lives dictated by an old, corrupt dictator. Nobody wants a single person making all of the decisions with no accountability. It is better to make decisions that influence our lives through democratic processes.

Dictatorships use fear to get obedience from people. They claim we must unite behind them to defeat the evil that threatens the homeland.

They say the threats are so bad they must control the media and lock up anyone who protests. Dictators use cultural, religious, and patriotic language to recruit the home team into accepting their "protective" care while ignoring their corruption and abuses.

One of the worst things about dictatorships is how popular they often are. People want to be protected. People want to feel safe. A sales pitch that incites fear and then promises safety and strength (to defeat "those people" by any means necessary) is often a sales pitch people will buy. We need to stop buying it. We can achieve our goals through peace rather than war. We can live in peaceful democratic republics with liberty and justice for all. We can achieve security for everyone by maintaining a peaceful and prosperous world.

We're transitioning from a world full of dictatorships to a world full of democracies. This is great for everyone, but it won't be easy. Dictators will do everything they can to hold onto power. Once a dictator is gone, building a functioning democratic republic and fair markets can take time.

The good news is that most people all over the world now support democratic forms of government. We're connecting with each other to share our thoughts and dreams. Most of us want democratic republics, fair markets, and sustainable environments. We want to pursue happiness with our loved ones in a safe, secure, and peaceful world.

We have so many advantages that prior generations didn't have. My younger brother is an engineer working on projects related to space exploration. He tries to solve engineering problems that most of us would conclude are impossible. He uses advanced tools and materials that were not available to engineers in prior decades. Engineers are making incredible advancements. The same is true with our pursuit of peace on Earth. Our tools are getting better as we continue to make progress.

Our advancements are gaining momentum. Markets help us trade with each other instead of invading each other. Democracies continue to sprout and bloom all over the world. Technology continues to advance. We have a global communications network for the first time in history. We have never had such an incredible opportunity to achieve peace on Earth!

Dictators will never support the goal of peace on Earth. They only support "peace" for themselves by controlling and conquering everything else. Their "conquer everything" plan always ends in costly disasters. We know there is a better way. We can live peacefully on this planet for many generations by supporting democratic republics, fair markets, and sustainable environments.

Since we are at the point in history when democracies are starting to outnumber dictatorships, we are also at the moment when peace on Earth becomes more likely. Democracies are more likely to pursue the goal of peace because it is the best option for all of us. There has never been a time in history when so many of us are free to pursue the goal of peace. Never before have we had so many organizations all over the world dedicated to finding sustainable and peaceful solutions to the problems we face on this planet.

Living in a democracy doesn't mean we will automatically achieve peace. Democracy gives us the option to choose peace, but it won't happen unless a majority of us are active for peace. Plenty of warmongers and wannabe dictators try to gain control of democratic nations to get wealth and power. Too many leaders have misled democratic nations into very costly wars. On the other hand, there are lots of democratic leaders who focus on building the foundations of peace through diplomacy, technology, and leadership. Elections make a difference. Our votes make a difference. Our decisions make a difference.

Dictators will try to stop the progress, but they will continue to fail. Dictatorships will continue to be replaced by democratic republics. Democratic republics will continue to give us incredible opportunities to achieve the goal of peace on Earth.

CHAPTER 28

MEDIA INFLUENCE

People spend a lot of time and money trying to influence our decisions. Politicians try to inspire us (or scare us) into voting for them. Companies want us to feel insecure about ourselves so we will buy their products to feel better. Religious leaders want us to fear eternal damnation so we will follow their rules. Lots of people are trying to influence our decisions every day.

Just a few decades ago, newspapers were the main source of news. Everyone got the same news. The stories were often from the viewpoint of the wealthy owner of the newspaper company. Now we have digital access to media outlets all over the world. We have access to great journalists, but we also have access to a lot of junk. Sometimes we think we know where information comes from, but then we find out it was a bunch of Russian agents trying to mislead us. Sometimes we think we know what happened, but then we find out we only heard one side of the story. What we see and hear daily influences the decisions we make.

In the summer of 2001, an eight-year-old boy was bitten by a shark in Florida. The story created great ratings for news channels. Journalists spent weeks covering the shark attack story. They also highlighted any other story that involved sharks that summer. People grew very concerned about shark attacks even though they were still very rare. There was no increase in the number of shark attacks that summer. The only thing that increased was the news coverage about shark attacks.

The same type of increased news coverage can influence our decisions when it comes to questions of war and peace. If we see scary images repeatedly, we might demand military action to protect us from those scary things. This type of propaganda technique has been used many times throughout history. Showing people the same images over and over again was easier when a few media outlets controlled everything we saw and heard. This is one reason dictators work so hard to maintain censorship and state media outlets in their countries.

Dictatorships have their propaganda outlets, but democratic republics have free and independent journalists. Russia censors information about their invasion of Ukraine, but I can instantly see an online post from a Ukrainian journalist. I rarely heard opposition to the wars in Iraq and Afghanistan on cable television in the United States, but I found online journalists teaching people the difference between the Shia, Sunni, and Kurdish populations in Iraq. We need to support open access to information so our decisions will continue to improve.

An entire generation went through an interesting media experiment when cable television was first invented. At first, cable television executives decided that many television channels would be split into topics such as news, sports, music, history, food, etc. After a few years, the cable executives decided the programs would be based on what people were most likely to watch. The music channel stopped playing music videos and started showing reality television programs. The news channels got higher ratings if they focused on crime and conflicts. The history channel got higher ratings by focusing on the history of war rather than the history of peace. What people saw on television was determined by decisions being made by cable television executives.

I noticed a few differences while looking for programs suitable for my children. The cable television channels for kids were full of commercials and programs filled with stupid humor (that we unanimously enjoyed). The public television channel had kids' educational programs. The programs on public television were never interrupted by loud, flashy commercials. If people only have access to commercial-based programs on cable television, they will have a distorted and limited perspective of reality. If people only access state media outlets, they will also have a distorted and limited version of reality.

Everything around us influences the information we have and the decisions we make. Changes in governments, technology, and business models end up changing the matrix of information we live within. Cable news channels don't want to risk advertising profits by opposing a national march to war. Media control in dictatorships is obvious, but we also need to consider the quality of information we receive while making decisions within democratic republics.

The internet has completely changed how we get information. Anyone from anywhere can post information. Local newspapers and corporate cable television lineups are no longer our only options. We went from three national television channels, to sixty cable television channels, to now having access to thousands of channels on the internet from all over the world. It's up to us to determine what we do with the ability to communicate with each other.

Corporate media doesn't like to focus on campaign finance reforms, but now we have the ability to communicate directly with each other. People living in rural areas only had access to AM radio stations dominated by conservative political programs. Now the internet allows people to hear different perspectives no matter where they live.

News channels often focus on stories about crime and violence. Seeing scary images every time we turn on the news can make us very anxious, depressed, and insecure. Fortunately, reality is way better than what we often see and hear. Many countries live in peace despite not being featured in the news. Media companies and politicians focus on our divisions, but we are united in so many ways. The vast majority of us agree that peace on Earth is the best strategy for our future. Most of us want to live in democratic republics rather than dictatorships. We all want our loved ones to live peacefully on this planet for many generations.

The best strategy for our own security is to support peace on Earth. We know how to live in peace. We have the tools to do it. Now we just need more of us to choose peace as our goal.

It's amazing to see online content being created by people all over the world. People no longer have to wait for approval from a dictator or a media executive before publishing something. Millions of people are singing, writing, and making videos about peaceful topics. We need millions of people creating peaceful content so some of it will go viral and influence the course of history.

Many people try to influence our decisions because our decisions impact the future. Our democratic republics and market economies are driven by the decisions we all make. Having a global communications network for the first time in history leads to better decisions. Having more democratic republics leads to better decisions. We see rapid advancements in many areas. History is a story of progress that continues today and into the future. Life on Earth is getting better.

CHAPTER 29

NOBEL PEACE PRIZE

Can you imagine how great life on Earth would be if millions of people tried to win the Nobel Peace Prize? Most people who win the Nobel Peace Prize were just doing what they thought was correct. Their efforts went viral to the point of being noticed by the Nobel Peace Prize committee. It's great to have a highly regarded prize awarded to people who contribute to the goal of peace on Earth.

Dmitry Muratov and Maria Ressa won the Nobel Peace Prize in 2021 for promoting freedom of the press and democracy. Dmitry Muratov is a journalist in Russia and the cofounder of a publication that is critical of the Russian dictatorship. Putin's cronies murdered many journalists who wrote for the publication. In 2022, Dmitry Muratov opposed his country's invasion of Ukraine. He auctioned off his Nobel Peace Prize medal and raised $103 million, which he donated to Ukrainian relief efforts. Maria Ressa is a journalist in the Philippines, where she has worked to expose corruption and the influence of harassment and false information. These journalists are making a difference in moving their countries from dictatorships to democracies. It is great to have the Nobel Peace Prize amplify their efforts.

In 2014, the Nobel Peace Prize was awarded to Kailash Satyarthi and Malala Yousafzai. Kailash Satyarthi is a children's rights activist in India who organized a global march to oppose child labor. Malala Yousafzai grew up in an area of Pakistan where religious extremists burned down schools for girls. She became famous for standing up to the religious extremists by saying all children should have access to education. We need millions of people standing up for children's rights, so lots of us will be in the right place at the right time to help make a difference.

President Obama won the Nobel Peace Prize shortly after taking office in 2009. Some people said he hadn't done anything yet, but he defeated the Republicans who had been invading and occupying other countries for the prior eight years. The rest of the world was relieved. They gave President Obama the Nobel Peace Prize for defeating the Republican warmongers. While President Obama still protected the United States with active military engagements, he greatly reduced the costs, deaths, and number of troops in combat by the time he left office.

In 2001, the Nobel Peace Prize was awarded to the United Nations. The United Nations is where the world gathers to discuss local, regional, and global issues in a peaceful forum. Having an open forum for discussing and resolving issues is a step toward a more peaceful planet. The United Nations has done a great job advocating for human rights around the world.

Nelson Mandela won the Nobel Peace Prize in 1993. Mandela was imprisoned for twenty-seven years because he wanted to end the terrible injustices of apartheid in South Africa. He helped move his nation from a system of institutionalized racial segregation to a democratic republic that protects the rights of everyone. He shared the Nobel Peace Prize with the president of South Africa, F.W. de

Klerk, who released Nelson Mandela from prison while working to dismantle apartheid in South Africa. Nelson Mandela then served as South Africa's president from 1994 to 1999.

I was very happy when I realized Russian leader Mikhail Gorbachev was a peaceful leader. I grew up thinking we might go to war with the Soviet Union. I didn't want my dad to die in a war, but it seemed like we would all die since both sides had a lot of nuclear weapons. Gorbachev started to move Russia from being a dictatorship to a democratic republic. Former Soviet republics became their own nations, and Germany was finally reunited after being split into East and West Germany for many decades. Unfortunately, Vladimir Putin became the leader of Russia a few years later. Putin used the economic struggles during the transition as an excuse to end many of the democratic reforms. Gorbachev continued to promote democracy and human rights after he left office. He won the Nobel Peace Prize in 1990.

Most of us will never win the Nobel Peace Prize, but we all have the ability to make a difference in our own unique ways. Some people save children by becoming foster parents. Some people volunteer as tutors and coaches. A friend of mine picks up trash around his neighborhood once a month. We can all get involved in helping make the world a better place.

Great organizations all over the world need volunteers. If you don't have time to volunteer, send a donation to ensure organizations have the necessary resources to improve the world. Consider working at a nonprofit organization when you're looking for a job. Post links on social media to donation pages for worthy causes.

Since we're at a point in history when democracies are becoming more common than dictatorships, we can support the democratic movement by making it a goal to vote in every election. Most states have online portals where you can check your voter registration and see when and where the next election is. Put the date of the election on your calendar.

As we move forward, we need to strengthen our democratic republics. It should be easy to vote but hard to cheat. Government meetings and actions should be open to the public. Journalists should be free to write what they want. These hallmarks of democratic governments will not be given to us. We must demand and protect the legitimacy of our democratic republics.

Not everyone will want to get involved with politics beyond voting. Some people will focus on protecting the environment. Some people will focus on reducing poverty. Fixing a broken swing at the playground also makes the world better. We need many people doing many different things to make the world a better place. Peace is active, and we all play a role. No action is too small. Each peaceful action is added to the peaceful steps being taken by billions of people all over the world.

Some of us might want to change things very quickly. However, the path to a peaceful existence won't be achieved through violence. Dictators thrive in violent and chaotic situations. They want people to feel scared. They want situations where they can unleash their weapons and brutality.

Many years ago, hundreds of thousands of people peacefully marched in Seattle for a clean planet. Still, the media focused on a few violent anarchists throwing rocks and causing damage. We must ensure our protests remain nonviolent if we want the media to focus on our message. Otherwise, violence is all the media will focus on. No matter how mad we are, how hurt we are, or how excited we are for a better future, we need to remain peaceful as we move toward our goals. We must put our energy into winning elections and making improvements without violence.

Lots of people will follow our example, especially children. If we reject violence, they will too. If we treat everyone with respect, they will too. If we take education seriously, they will too. If we vote, they will too. We can make the world a better place by setting a good example. The same is true with our friends and coworkers.

We can also set a positive example as nations. The great thing about democratic republics is we can make improvements. We have the ability to kick warmongers out of office. We can make sure all children have access to education. We can pass campaign finance reforms. Everything we do sets an example for other people and other nations to follow. Let's make sure our national example is a peaceful one.

The Nobel Peace Prize committee will have many peaceful examples to choose from in future years. The battle between democracy and dictatorships will generate new heroes. One recent example is the president of Ukraine, Volodymyr Zelenskyy. He went from being an actor in comedy shows to being elected president of Ukraine. He then found himself leading a democratic nation to defend itself from the military onslaught of a brutal dictator trying to steal Ukraine's land and wealth. President Zelenskyy has led his nation with determination, patriotism, and courage. Ten years ago, nobody would have guessed he would become a hero in the global battle for democracy.

We never know how our actions will impact other people and the course of history. Maybe we'll make a difference by having something ripple through history in unexpected ways. For example, my wife told me small plastic particles are getting into our water, food, and bodies. Instead of sending a bunch of plastic drinking straws to the landfill after using them once, we started saying, "No straw please," while ordering drinks. We've been doing it for years. Between the two of us, we have stopped hundreds of straws from ending up in the landfill.

It's such a small and easy thing to do.

Can you imagine how much plastic would be kept out of landfills if someone reading this gets motivated to start an organization to reduce the use of plastic? Can you imagine if the organization convinced restaurants to save money and plastic by making straws available by request rather than by default? Can you imagine what would happen if the organization got a shoutout from a celebrity, which attracted media attention and lots of donations? Maybe a couple of years later, the organization would expand to promote health and wellness for people worldwide. Then perhaps the organization ends up winning a Nobel Peace Prize. It could happen.

I wasn't sure if a stay-at-home dad could influence a national presidential election, but my social media efforts went national a few weeks before the 2012 election. I wasn't sure if knocking on doors in my neighborhood could influence who my governor and president were, but a few votes in the swing state of Wisconsin could change the course of history. I wasn't sure if I could stop wars from happening, but millions of us campaigning and voting for President Obama probably stopped John McCain from sending more troops into Iraq, Afghanistan, Syria, Libya, and Iran.

If forty thousand Democrats in three swing states had stayed home instead of voting, Donald Trump would have won a second term as President of the United States. I never in a million years thought we would defeat a wannabe dictator in the United States of America by organizing a cast reunion of *The Princess Bride* movie in swing state Wisconsin. Voting makes a difference. Getting involved makes a difference. Supporting the goal of peace makes a difference.

CHAPTER 30

PEACE IS ACTIVE

There's no reason why we should be anything other than a peaceful community of friends. We're all very different, yet we're all basically the same. I don't know how we all got here or where we'll go after we leave, but we're all together now.

The human species has the ability to think. We all decide what we are going to do with ourselves on a daily basis. Communicating with each other gives us a better chance of making good decisions. Any suggestions we give each other will be appreciated, but our individual minds will ultimately make the decisions that shape our own lives and the course of history.

We all want stability. We all want things to be figured out so we can live a safe and peaceful life. Dictators promise life will be easier if we support them. Then they restrict access to information and use violence and corruption to stay in power. We don't have to live the same way we lived in the past. Many of us now support democratic forms of government. We can see life improving in so many ways.

Moving from dictatorships to democratic republics is a shift in how we approach our existence. Dictators want to conquer and control the rest of the world, but a growing majority of us are now using our democratic republics to pursue the goal of peace. Instead of conquering and controlling everything, we support peaceful, fair, and sustainable systems of life. This includes our governments and respect for the environmental foundations of our existence.

For thousands of generations, humanity enjoyed an abundant means of survival on Earth. Our population was small enough to survive and expand without weakening the balance of Earth's circle of life. By the time our population could be measured in the billions, maintaining our existence became more of a challenge. We discovered new farming methods to produce more food. We learned how to drill deeper into the planet to find water and fossil fuels. These advances allowed our population to keep growing, but the resources on this planet are limited. Now we're learning how to balance our existence within a healthy environment so we can live on this planet for many generations.

Fishing is a good example. Thousands of years ago, people living on this planet could eat as many fish as they wanted. The fish would reproduce and provide a constant source of food. However, as the human population expanded, more people caught and ate fish. The fish population was not able to reproduce fast enough. Some species of fish disappeared. Instead of depleting our resources, we're now making agreements and laws to use natural resources in sustainable ways.

We're making a lot of advances on this planet. We figured out specific chemicals were harming the atmosphere, so we banned the use of the chemicals. We figured out that burning fossil fuels is warming our planet, so we're switching to more sustainable forms of energy. We figured out population growth slows when more people have access to healthcare and education. We figured out that eating less meat is better for our bodies and the planet. We invented new water testing equipment to trace pollutants back to specific sources, improving our drinking water quality.

Scientists, teachers, leaders, mothers, fathers, sisters, and brothers are making the world better in their own unique ways. We can choose to support democratic forms of government. We can choose to support fair markets and sustainable environments. We can choose to be nice to each other and respect each other. We can choose to advance peacefully.

This doesn't mean we control everything with our choices. Many things happen naturally within our bodies we can't control. We don't consciously decide when new blood cells are created or when our heart beats. However, we can choose to put toxins into our bodies. If we harm our bodies, then the means of our survival will be damaged. Similarly, we can't control Earth's circle of life, but we can choose to pollute or deplete it. It's our choice to make.

Life on Earth will continue to change. Technology will continue to advance. Evolution will always progress, and our human decisions will influence its course. Peace on Earth is the best strategy for everyone.

We need people to be active for peace in every nation. A majority of us live in democracies for the first time in history. We have the freedom to speak out, create organizations, donate to good causes, mobilize voters, and educate our children. If we're going to achieve peace, we need to realize we're all on the same team. We can make life better for ourselves by joining billions of people worldwide who share the goal of peace.

Humans thought Earth was flat for ninety-nine percent of our history. Now we have a picture of our planet taken from the moon. Our ancestors thought gods filled the heavens above the clouds. Now we have telescopes that reveal distant galaxies. We have refrigerators, movies, and microwaves. Our ancestors would be so jealous. Life is so much better than it was for prior generations. Our standard of living continues to improve. Our access to information continues to expand. We don't have to live the way we did in the past.

Since I was five years old, peace on Earth has been my goal. Growing up in a military family gave me a peaceful purpose in life. I wasn't sure if I could make a difference, but I found out I could by being a good citizen in my community, by voting, and by getting involved. I've tried to be a positive addition to this planet.

I'm writing this story as an example of someone active for peace. We all have the ability to live on a peaceful and healthy planet. The choice is ours to make. We, the people, get to decide. I invite you to join billions of us who support the goal of peace on Earth. We're closer to the goal than any generation before us. Peace is active, not passive. Do something to make the world a more peaceful place. Be a positive addition to this planet. Thank you.

ABOUT THE AUTHOR

Tom McCann lives in Madison, Wisconsin with his wife and two children. Tom grew up in Eau Claire, Wisconsin and graduated from the University of Wisconsin—Madison. Tom spent a few years building travel websites while living in the Colorado Rocky Mountains. After moving back to Madison, Tom started volunteering and working for the Democratic Party of Wisconsin.

Printed in the United States
by Baker & Taylor Publisher Services